SLOW COOKER FAMILY FAVORITES

SLOW COOKER FAMILY FAVORITES

CLASSIC MEALS YOU'LL WANT TO SHARE

MAGGIE SHI

THE COUNTRYMAN PRESS

A division of W. W. Norton & Company

Independent Publishers Since 1923

For information about permission to reproduce selections from this book, write to Permissions,
The Countryman Press, 500 Fifth Avenue, New York, NY 10110

For information about special discounts for bulk purchases, please contact
W. W. Norton Special Sales at specialsales@wwnorton.com or 800-233-4830

Book design by Nina LoSchiavo
Manufacturing by RR Donnelley, Shenzhen

Library of Congress Cataloging-in-Publication Data

Names: Shi, Maggie, author.
Title: Slow Cooker Family Favorites : Classic Meals You'll Want to Share / Maggie Shi.
Description: Woodstock, VT : Countryman Press, a division of W. W. Norton & Company, Independent Publishers Since 1923, [2016] | Includes index. Identifiers: LCCN 2016013902 | ISBN 9781581573459 (pbk.)
Subjects: LCSH: Electric cooking, Slow. | LCGFT: Cookbooks. Classification: LCC TX827 .S5324 2016 | DDC 641.5/884—dc23
LC record available at https://lccn.loc.gov/2016013902

The Countryman Press
www.countrymanpress.com

A division of W. W. Norton & Company, Inc.
500 Fifth Avenue, New York, NY 10110
www.wwnorton.com

10 9 8 7 6 5 4 3 2 1

To Mom and Dad.

CONTENTS

INTRODUCTION

I've always loved hosting gatherings and parties. When I graduated from college and moved into my own apartment in New York City, one of my very first acts as a real "grownup" was to throw a housewarming party. (Sure, I might have forgotten to have ice on hand for the drinks, but who really cared?) My annual holiday party quickly became famous for its crispy bacon-wrapped dates stuffed with hunks of Parmesan and slow-simmered mulled wine. My friends always have a blast customizing their own drinks at the do-it-yourself Bloody Mary bar I set up for my casual buffet-style Sunday brunches. Every month, a group of women gathers over wine and snacks in my apartment to discuss the latest book we've read (or haven't read, in some cases). Inviting people into my home is fun for me; I love to turn any event (for example, a vacation to Paris) into an excuse to host a gathering (French cheese and macarons smuggled back in my carry-on, along with sausages, baguettes, kirs, and Lillet). For me, spending time with friends and family in my home always involves spoiling them with good food and drinks.

The slow cooker, however, didn't figure into my life until much later. When I first moved to New York, I resisted getting a slow cooker. While everyone seemed to love this appliance—"Just set it and forget it!"—and I was eager to play around with it, I couldn't justify yet another object cluttering up the limited countertop space in my typically tiny New York kitchen. But while working for *Real Simple* magazine's website, I helped research and write a roundup of slow cooker models. Somehow, I managed to acquire not one, but three.

My early experiments with the slow cooker were pretty typical—stews and soups. The very first results, however, were not too promising. While I loved the concept—a little prep, toss everything into the cooker, carry on with your life for a few hours, then return to a delicious-smelling home and an even more mouthwateringly good one-pot meal—when I finally dug into those first couple dishes, they didn't taste as their aromas promised. The results were always more watery than expected, the flavors muddled. While they smelled amazing, they tasted mediocre.

I quickly learned that slow cooking takes a bit of finesse. You may need to add an extra ingredient or two to amp up the flavor, or have a heavier hand with the salt and seasonings. Adding fresh herbs or some kind of acid at the end is often essential to livening up the dish. And letting the results sit for a little while before serving often works wonders to

absorb excess moisture or thicken liquids. (You can find more tips in the Slow Cooker Tips and Tricks section, page xvii.)

Once you've got it figured out, the slow cooker is indeed a wondrous thing. I admit, I tend to be a bit lazy when it comes to cooking; I will sometimes buy spaghetti sauce in a jar or prepared pesto instead of making my own from scratch. Let's face it—most of us just don't have that kind of time. Cooking in a slow cooker is meant to make life easier, more convenient, or to save you time—or all three. Therefore, I've tried to keep the recipes in this book as simple as possible. I—like you, probably—hate to add extra steps to any recipe. That said, there are a few dishes in this book that do require some pre- or post-cooking, such as browning meat or reducing a sauce. I've tried to keep those to a minimum and only include such steps when I think it makes a big difference in the outcome.

While I'm not one of those "everything from scratch" people, I do try to keep my intake of overly processed and packaged foods to a minimum. I've tried to keep everything as fresh as possible in this book, but again, there are exceptions. Some slow cooker recipes just work better when using condensed cheese soup or instant rice (ingredients I would ordinarily shun). And again, in the interest of making life easier, I'm not going to require you to make your own Buffalo sauce or green chili enchilada sauce from scratch. The slow cooker should be a convenience, not a nuisance. When buying pre-packaged ingredients, I do always try to buy the highest quality I can afford, with a minimum of additives and no artificial colors or flavors. (Whole Foods and I became best friends while I was writing this book.)

If you've bought this book, it's likely you already own a slow cooker. But most people I know use theirs solely for chilis, stews, and soups. Once you've tried some of the recipes in this book and expanded your horizons (Cheesecake! Hot chocolate! Dinner rolls!), you'll be amazed at just how versatile this appliance can be.

WHY USE A SLOW COOKER?

In this book, you'll find main dishes and sides, of course, but also lots of other festive food you might not initially think of making in a slow cooker, including dips, desserts, and drinks. You might ask, "Why would anyone make spinach dip or chocolate cake or warm punch in the slow cooker, when it could just as easily be made on the stovetop or in the oven?" For one thing, using the slow cooker frees up space in your kitchen. At Thanksgiving, for example, you can easily cook mashed potatoes in your slow cooker, which makes another burner on your stove available. Need to bake two things in the oven at once, but at different temperatures? Try baking one in the slow cooker instead. (Stuffing, rolls, and cakes can all be made in the slow cooker.) Another bonus: The slow cooker will keep your food warm for hours. You don't need to worry about reheating the buttered carrots or wonder if the meatballs are getting cold. Warm dips and drinks, of course, are ideal for slow cooker entertaining. Hosting a gathering or family dinner on a weeknight becomes a lot easier, too. No time to pull together an entire meal after work? You can put all your ingredients in the slow cooker in the morning, let it cook all day, then come home and serve your family and guests a warm pot of Smoky Beef Chili (page 79) for dinner, or an elegant dish of Wine-Poached Pears (page 111) for dessert.

Mainly, though, using the slow cooker for all kinds of meals and celebrations is just a lot of fun. There's not one person who isn't impressed when I tell them that the Chocolate Chip Cheesecake (page 122) they're eating was made in the slow cooker, or that the Honey Bourbon Cider (page 138) they're sipping on was concocted in a slow cooker. Using the slow cooker in unexpected ways is a great way to get the conversation going!

This book contains recipes perfect for all kinds of gatherings, whether it's a holiday like Christmas or St. Patrick's Day, a birthday or cocktail party, or just the first time the family has been able to sit down together for dinner in a week. Some of the most important parts of a meal or celebration are for everyone to be able to relax, eat, drink, and spend time together—and with the low-effort, make-ahead slow cooker, even the host can sit back and enjoy the moment.

SLOW COOKER TIPS AND TRICKS

To make the most of your slow cooker, you need to get to know it very well. One of the challenges with creating slow cooker recipes is that every appliance is different—different models and brands cook at various heat levels, so it's important to know how your slow cooker works. For example, I have three slow cookers—two are the same brand (thought not the same model), and one is a different brand. I quickly realized that one of them tended to cook hotter than the others, and also cooked unevenly—one side of whatever I was cooking would often get scorched. So now I know that I can only use it for certain dishes, like soups or drinks, that won't burn. One easy way to test your slow cooker's effectiveness is to bake something in it. If you can bake a cake successfully in your slow cooker and it doesn't scorch or cook unevenly, you know you have a reliable, efficient appliance. And if you know your slow cooker tends to cook on the hotter or cooler side, you can adjust recipe cooking times to get the best results.

I used a 6-quart oval slow cooker for all these recipes; I think it's the ideal size if you're cooking for a crowd, and the oval shape (as opposed to a round shape) more easily accommodates large items like pot roasts and turkey breasts. If you have a smaller slow cooker in addition to a large one, by all means use it for the dips and some of the appetizers and desserts. However, the recipes should all turn out well in the 6-quart cooker.

One more note about your choice of slow cooker: Make sure your model has an automatic timer that switches to "warming" mode when the cooking time is done. In my opinion, there is absolutely no point in having a slow cooker if you need to physically be present to shut the appliance off when time is up. You need to be able to add your ingredients, turn the slow cooker on, and then walk away—go to work, run errands, spend time with friends, see a movie—and have peace of mind that the slow cooker will turn off and keep your food warm until you're ready to eat.

For optimal results, keep these additional tips and tricks in mind when using your slow cooker:

DON'T BE SHY WITH THE SALT AND SEASONINGS.

You might be surprised at some of the quantities in the recipes in this book. (One whole tablespoon of salt?) In the slow cooker, flavors can get muddled; the ingredients cook for a long time at a low, steady heat, so they don't get a chance to reduce and concentrate. So you'll need to amp up the flavor with slightly larger quantities of herbs and spices than you'd normally use. And that leads to . . .

ALWAYS TASTE THE DISH BEFORE SERVING, AND ADD MORE SALT OR SEASONINGS IF NEEDED.

This rule actually holds true for any dish you cook, but it's especially important to remember when slow cooking. Taste the dish when it's done, and even if you've already added the quantity of salt called for in the recipe, add more if you think it's necessary. Recipe quantities—particularly savory ones—are meant to be a guideline. For some people, 1 teaspoon of salt might be plenty. Maybe you're adding a milder sausage than I used, or the brand of broth you're using contains less salt than the one your neighbor is using. Adjust the seasonings according to your taste preferences; there's no wrong answer.

ADD FRESH HERBS, GARNISHES, OR ACIDS BEFORE SERVING TO BOOST THE FLAVOR.

Many of the recipes in this book call for some kind of final stir-in or garnish—chopped parsley or cilantro, sliced scallions, a squeeze of fresh lemon, a tablespoon of vinegar. As I mentioned before, some slow cooker dishes, especially stews, can taste a little watered down and muddy by the time they're done. A little bit of freshness or acid can make all the difference in the world when it comes to brightening up flavors and making the ingredients sing.

IF THE DISH SEEMS TOO WATERY OR MOIST WHEN IT'S DONE, REMOVE THE LID AND LET IT SIT FOR ABOUT 20 MINUTES.

Your food won't get cold because the slow cooker is on "warming" mode, but removing the lid while the insert is still hot lets some of that extra liquid inside evaporate. If it's a stew, stir up the ingredients and then let them sit to thicken the sauce slightly. Similarly, if it's a cake or some other dish that involves bread or baked goods and it seems slightly underdone (the "clean toothpick" test usually doesn't work with slow cooker recipes), letting it sit uncovered for 20 minutes will leave you with a dish that's still moist but not overly soupy.

DON'T BE TEMPTED TO SUBSTITUTE LOW-FAT OR FAT-FREE VERSIONS OF INGREDIENTS.

I freely admit that the recipes in this book are not intended to be healthy. It's tempting to want to swap in low-fat cream cheese or fat-free milk in some of these recipes in order to cut back on the fat or calories, but resist the temptation. Using low-fat or fat-free versions—especially when you're working with a bunch of dairy ingredients that need to meld together—can cause curdling. The results are unappetizing to look at and to eat. Go ahead and indulge; these recipes are meant for festive occasions, not for everyday eating. Throw a party with Cheesy Bacon Dip (page 2) and S'mores Casserole (page 120) one night, and eat salmon and veggies for dinner the next night. It's all about moderation, not deprivation.

THE LOW SETTING GENERALLY YIELDS THE BEST RESULTS.

When given an option, I try to cook on low whenever possible. I find that dishes cook better on a gentler, longer heat. There are, however, many dishes that benefit from cooking on high; when I haven't offered a low alternative, that means that I think the high setting is important for optimal results. If you're short on time, of course, go for the high setting and adjust the time accordingly. (As a general rule, cut the cooking time in half if you're cooking on high.)

TRIM OFF ANY FAT ON MEAT BEFORE ADDING TO THE SLOW COOKER.

The more fat that's left on the meat, the oilier the resulting sauce will be, because it renders out into the stew—you can't drain it off at the end the way you would if you were sautéing meat in a skillet. So be sure to trim away any extra fat if you're not browning the meat first.

CHAPTER 1

DIPS

CHEESY BACON DIP

~

SERVES **12** TO **14** • SLOW COOKER TIME **2** TO **3** HOURS

Unsurprisingly, cheese and bacon are two of my favorite foods. (I suspect I'm not the only one.) This dip combines gooey, melted cheddar with meaty, salty bacon—who can resist? I like to add half the bacon at the start of the recipe to infuse all the ingredients with savory, smoky flavor, then stir in the remaining bacon at the end to retain its crispness. Garnishing with sliced scallions helps bring some freshness to this admittedly decadent dip.

2 (8-OUNCE) PACKAGES CREAM CHEESE, SOFTENED AND CUBED

4 CUPS SHREDDED CHEDDAR CHEESE

1 CUP HEAVY CREAM

1 TABLESPOON WORCESTERSHIRE SAUCE

1 TEASPOON ONION POWDER

1 TEASPOON PREPARED MUSTARD

16 SLICES BACON, COOKED AND CRUMBLED, DIVIDED

SLICED SCALLIONS, FOR GARNISH

TORTILLA CHIPS OR BAGUETTE SLICES, FOR SERVING

In a slow cooker, stir together the cream cheese, cheddar, cream, Worcestershire, onion powder, mustard, and half the bacon.

Cover and cook on low for 2 to 3 hours, or until the cheeses have melted.

Stir in the remaining cooked bacon, making sure all the ingredients are well-combined, and sprinkle sliced scallions on top. Serve with tortilla chips or baguette slices.

CREAMY GARLIC DIP

~

SERVES **8** TO **10** • SLOW COOKER TIME **3** TO **4 HOURS**

Cream cheese, mayo, sour cream . . . I admit, this dip doesn't sound like the healthiest or the most sophisticated one around, but it's absolutely addictive—trust me! Once you start eating it, you won't be able to stop. To make short work of prepping the garlic, I like to smash all the cloves, remove the peels, and go to town with my chef's knife. If you have one of those handy garlic chopper tools, by all means, use it.

2 (8-OUNCE) PACKAGES CREAM CHEESE, SOFTENED AND CUBED

⅔ CUP MAYONNAISE

¼ CUP SOUR CREAM

1 WHOLE HEAD GARLIC, PEELED AND MINCED

¼ CUP CHOPPED FRESH PARSLEY

CRACKERS OR CRUDITÉS, FOR DIPPING

In a slow cooker, stir together the cream cheese, mayonnaise, sour cream, and garlic.

Cover and cook on low for 3 to 4 hours, or until the cheese has melted and the garlic has mellowed.

Stir in the parsley, making sure all the ingredients are well-combined. Serve with crackers or crudités.

CARAMELIZED ONION DIP

~

SERVES **10** TO **12** • SLOW COOKER TIME **2** TO **3** HOURS

Cooking the onions before adding them to the slow cooker requires a bit of extra work, but it's definitely necessary (and worth it) in this recipe. The onions become meltingly soft, sweet, and nutty as they slowly caramelize; they're the star of the dish, so don't skip this step.

1 TABLESPOON BUTTER

1 TABLESPOON OLIVE OIL

3 SWEET ONIONS, SUCH AS VIDALIA, THINLY SLICED INTO HALF-MOONS

1 (8-OUNCE) PACKAGE CREAM CHEESE, SOFTENED AND CUBED

½ CUP MAYONNAISE

2 CUPS SHREDDED CHEDDAR CHEESE

2 CUPS SHREDDED MOZZARELLA CHEESE

3 SCALLIONS, SLICED

TRISCUITS OR BAGUETTE SLICES, FOR SERVING

In a large skillet, melt the butter with olive oil over medium heat. Add the onions and cook, stirring occasionally, until the onions are tender and caramelized, about 20 minutes.

In a slow cooker, stir together the cream cheese, mayonnaise, cheddar, mozzarella, scallions, and caramelized onions.

Cover and cook on low for 2 to 3 hours, or until the cheeses have melted. Stir thoroughly, making sure all the ingredients are well-combined, and serve with Triscuits or baguette slices.

NEW ENGLAND CLAM DIP

~

SERVES **8** TO **10** • SLOW COOKER TIME **2** TO **3 HOURS**

I have friends who can't stop raving about this dip. It's super rich, bursting with clams, and has a nice bit of heat from the Tabasco. I like to serve it with potato chips to mimic the potatoes you'll find in a traditional New England clam chowder. Keep a bottle of Tabasco on the side if some guests want it extra hot; the spice helps cut through the richness of the cream cheese and makes this dip even more delicious.

2 (8-OUNCE) PACKAGES CREAM CHEESE, SOFTENED AND CUBED

¼ CUP SOUR CREAM

3 (6.5-OUNCE) CANS CHOPPED CLAMS, DRAINED

3 SCALLIONS, SLICED AND DIVIDED

3 SLICES BACON, COOKED AND CRUMBLED

2 TEASPOONS WORCESTERSHIRE SAUCE

1 TABLESPOON TABASCO SAUCE, PLUS MORE FOR SERVING

1 TABLESPOON UNSALTED BUTTER, MELTED

½ CUP OYSTER CRACKERS, CRUSHED

POTATO CHIPS, FOR SERVING

In a slow cooker, stir together the cream cheese, sour cream, clams, 2 sliced scallions, bacon, Worcestershire, and Tabasco.

Cover and cook on low for 2 to 3 hours, or until the cream cheese has melted.

Meanwhile, in a small bowl, mix the melted butter with the crushed oyster crackers and 1 sliced scallion.

When the dip is done, stir thoroughly, making sure all the ingredients are well-combined. Sprinkle the oyster cracker mixture over the top. Serve with potato chips and extra Tabasco on the side.

MARYLAND CRAB DIP

~

SERVES **8** TO **10** • SLOW COOKER TIME **2** TO **3** HOURS

I love crab, but cracking the shells and digging out tiny bits of meat is more work than I'm willing to put in. With this recipe, you get to enjoy all that tasty meat with very little effort. Sweet, juicy hunks of crab matched with spicy Old Bay is a deservedly classic pairing. The corn kernels provide little pops of sweetness and add a pretty color to this luscious dip—one of my favorites in this book.

2 (8-OUNCE) PACKAGES CREAM CHEESE, SOFTENED AND CUBED

½ CUP GRATED PARMESAN CHEESE

½ CUP MAYONNAISE

1 TABLESPOON WORCESTERSHIRE SAUCE

2 TABLESPOONS OLD BAY SEASONING

1 CUP FINELY CHOPPED WHITE OR VIDALIA ONION

3 CLOVES GARLIC, MINCED

1 POUND CRABMEAT, DRAINED AND PICKED THROUGH

½ CUP CORN, FRESH OR FROZEN AND THAWED

CRACKERS, FOR SERVING

In a slow cooker, stir together the cream cheese, Parmesan, mayonnaise, Worcestershire, Old Bay, onion, and garlic. Stir in the crabmeat and corn.

Cover and cook on low for 2 to 3 hours, or until the cheese has melted. Stir thoroughly, making sure all the ingredients are well-combined. Serve with crackers.

SPINACH-PARMESAN DIP

~

SERVES **6** TO **8** • SLOW COOKER TIME **1** TO **2 HOURS**

I used to serve spinach dip made with powdered soup mix in a bread bowl serving dish at my parties. I've nixed the packaged mix, added Parmesan and mozzarella, and now serve it directly in the slow cooker so it stays warm throughout the night. Everyone loves a good spinach dip, and this one is no exception. There's basically no prep, so it comes together in a jiffy.

1¼ CUPS SOUR CREAM

½ TEASPOON GARLIC POWDER

1 (10-OUNCE) PACKAGE FROZEN CHOPPED SPINACH, THAWED AND EXCESS MOISTURE SQUEEZED OUT

½ CUP GRATED PARMESAN CHEESE

2 CUPS SHREDDED MOZZARELLA CHEESE

BAKED PITA CHIPS, CRACKERS, OR CRUDITÉS

In a slow cooker, stir together the sour cream, garlic powder, spinach, Parmesan, and mozzarella.

Cover and cook on low for 1 to 2 hours, or until the cheeses have melted. Stir thoroughly, making sure all the ingredients are well-combined. Serve with the baked pita chips, crackers, or crudités.

CHEESY MEXICAN BEAN DIP

~

SERVES **10** TO **12** • SLOW COOKER TIME **1 HOUR 30 MINUTES**

This recipe is loosely based on classic seven-layer dip. There's tons of cheese, sour cream, refried beans, and some chipotle chiles to add a subtle smoky heat. You can customize it with additional ingredients if you like: sliced black olives, salsa, and additional hot sauce would all be great add-ins. Though it's tasty, it's not the most attractive dip, but you'll sprinkle extra cheese and scallions on top before serving to help make this dip look as good as it tastes.

1   (8-OUNCE) PACKAGE CREAM CHEESE, SOFTENED AND CUBED

1   CUP SOUR CREAM

1   (16-OUNCE) CAN REFRIED BEANS

1   CHIPOTLE CHILE IN ADOBO SAUCE, CHOPPED

1   (1.4-OUNCE) PACKAGE TACO SEASONING

2   CUPS SHREDDED CHEDDAR CHEESE, DIVIDED

2   CUPS SHREDDED MONTEREY JACK CHEESE, DIVIDED

2   SCALLIONS, SLICED

    TORTILLA CHIPS, FOR SERVING

In a slow cooker, stir together the cream cheese, sour cream, refried beans, chipotle, taco seasoning, 1 cup cheddar, and 1 cup Monterey Jack.

Cover and cook on high for 1½ hours, or until the cheeses have melted. Stir thoroughly, making sure all the ingredients are well-combined. Top with the remaining 1 cup cheddar and 1 cup Monterey Jack and sprinkle with the scallions. When the cheese has melted, serve with tortilla chips.

SPICY BEAN DIP

~

Since you're already getting a dose of heat from two chipotles, I like to use a mild salsa in this recipe to better control the level of spice. But if you like it hot, by all means, go for a hotter salsa. The corn and bell peppers provide a nice texture, color, and slight sweetness.

1 (16-OUNCE) CAN REFRIED BEANS

1 (15-OUNCE) CAN BLACK BEANS, RINSED AND DRAINED

1 CUP CORN, FRESH OR FROZEN AND THAWED

1 CUP DICED RED BELL PEPPER

1 CUP MILD SALSA

2 CHIPOTLE CHILES IN ADOBO SAUCE, CHOPPED, PLUS 2 TEASPOONS ADOBO SAUCE

1½ CUPS SHREDDED CHEDDAR, MONTEREY JACK, OR PEPPER JACK CHEESE, DIVIDED

4 SCALLIONS, SLICED

TORTILLA CHIPS, FOR SERVING

In a slow cooker, combine the refried beans, black beans, corn, bell pepper, salsa, chipotles, adobo sauce, and 1 cup of cheese. Stir gently to combine.

Cover and cook on low for 3 hours, or until the cheese has melted and the bell pepper is tender.

Stir the dip, then sprinkle with the scallions and remaining ½ cup cheese. When the cheese has melted, serve with tortilla chips.

ARTICHOKE-RED PEPPER DIP

~

SERVES **8** TO **10** • SLOW COOKER TIME **2** TO **3 HOURS**

For a twist on the usual artichoke dip, toss in some chopped roasted red peppers: They add a dash of bright color and just a hint of smokiness. Don't be tempted to lighten up this recipe by substituting low-fat versions of the sour cream, milk, or cream cheese. You need the richness of the real thing to help bind all the ingredients together smoothly.

1   (8-OUNCE) PACKAGE CREAM CHEESE, SOFTENED AND CUBED

½   CUP SOUR CREAM

½   CUP MAYONNAISE

½   WHITE ONION, FINELY CHOPPED

1   GARLIC CLOVE, MINCED

¼   CUP GRATED PARMESAN CHEESE

1   CUP SHREDDED MONTEREY JACK CHEESE

1   (20-OUNCE) JAR ROASTED RED PEPPERS, DRAINED, EXCESS MOISTURE SQUEEZED OUT, AND CHOPPED

1   (14-OUNCE) CAN ARTICHOKE HEARTS IN WATER, DRAINED AND CHOPPED

CRACKERS, FOR SERVING

In a slow cooker, stir together the cream cheese, sour cream, mayonnaise, onion, garlic, and Parmesan. Stir in the Monterey Jack, roasted red peppers, and artichoke hearts.

Cover and cook on low for 2 to 3 hours, or until the cheeses have melted. Stir thoroughly, making sure all the ingredients are well-combined, and serve with crackers.

PIZZA DIP

~

SERVES **8** TO **10** • SLOW COOKER TIME **1** TO **2 HOURS**

I first stumbled across pizza dip when I was testing recipes for a website. Since then, I've made countless versions of it, and it's universally adored. After all, everyone loves pizza—who could resist pizza in dip form? This recipe is fun because you can vary it according to your pizza topping preferences. Substitute cooked crumbled sausage in place of the pepperoni, swap in ham and pineapple, or use whatever you love best.

2 (8-OUNCE) PACKAGES CREAM CHEESE, SOFTENED AND CUBED

1 (15-OUNCE) CAN PIZZA SAUCE

½ CUP GRATED PARMESAN CHEESE

2 CUPS SHREDDED MOZZARELLA CHEESE

½ CUP CHOPPED PEPPERONI

½ CUP PITTED BLACK OLIVES, SLICED

½ GREEN BELL PEPPER, DICED

BAGUETTE SLICES OR BAGEL CHIPS, FOR SERVING

In a slow cooker, place the cream cheese cubes in an even layer. Pour the pizza sauce on top. Sprinkle evenly with the Parmesan, mozzarella, pepperoni, olives, and bell pepper.

Cover and cook on low for 1 to 2 hours, or until the cheeses have melted. Serve with baguette slices or bagel chips.

SOUTHWESTERN CHICKEN DIP

≈

SERVES **10** TO **12** • SLOW COOKER TIME **2** TO **3 HOURS**

If you have leftovers from last night's roast, this is a great way to use up extra cooked chicken. This hearty dip eats almost like a meal; you could even use it to top pasta or on sliced bread for open-face sandwiches.

1 (8-OUNCE) PACKAGE CREAM CHEESE, SOFTENED AND CUBED

2 CUPS SOUR CREAM

1 (4-OUNCE) CAN DICED GREEN CHILES

2 CUPS SHREDDED PEPPER JACK CHEESE

3 CUPS SHREDDED COOKED CHICKEN

2 RED BELL PEPPERS, DICED

1 YELLOW ONION, DICED

1 TABLESPOON ONION POWDER

1 TABLESPOON GARLIC POWDER

2 TEASPOONS SALT

TORTILLA CHIPS OR BAGUETTE SLICES, FOR SERVING

In a slow cooker, stir together the cream cheese, sour cream, green chiles, cheese, chicken, peppers, onion, onion powder, garlic powder, and salt.

Cover and cook on low for 2 to 3 hours, or until the cheeses have melted and the peppers and onion are tender. Stir thoroughly, making sure all the ingredients are well-combined, and serve with tortilla chips or baguette slices.

MARINARA DIPPING SAUCE

~

SERVES **10** TO **12** • SLOW COOKER TIME **7 HOURS**

This amazing, almost-no-effort tomato sauce simmers for hours to create a versatile, complex sauce with layers of flavor that's one of the best I've ever tasted. It makes a great party dip for all kinds of breads, but it works just as well as a sauce for pasta. You can also serve it with my Meatball Sliders (page 26). No matter how you use it, you'll be licking your plate clean to get every last drop.

2 TABLESPOONS EXTRA-VIRGIN OLIVE OIL

2 TABLESPOONS TOMATO PASTE

1 TABLESPOON RED WINE VINEGAR

3 LARGE FRESH BASIL SPRIGS

2 GARLIC CLOVES, MINCED

2 (28-OUNCE) CANS CRUSHED TOMATOES

2 TEASPOONS SALT, PLUS MORE IF NEEDED

BREADSTICKS, GARLIC BREAD, OR BAGUETTE SLICES, FOR SERVING

In a slow cooker, stir together the oil, tomato paste, vinegar, basil, garlic, tomatoes, and salt.

Cover and cook on low for 7 hours. Taste for seasoning. Serve with breadsticks, garlic bread, or baguette slices for dipping.

APPETIZERS & PARTY SNACKS

BUFFALO CHICKEN MEATBALLS

~

SERVES **8** • SLOW COOKER TIME **1 HOUR 30 MINUTES**

I love reinventing a classic dish in a different form (see my Pizza Dip, page 17), so this recipe was a lot of fun to create. I've incorporated some essential Buffalo chicken accompaniments—chopped celery and crumbled blue cheese—directly inside each meatball, so you'll get a well-rounded bite every time. I like to use my hands to mix the ground chicken with the other ingredients; it's gentler than using a spoon, and your hands are going to get dirty anyway when you form the meatballs!

1   POUND GROUND CHICKEN

½   CUP PANKO BREADCRUMBS

1   LARGE EGG

½   TEASPOON GARLIC POWDER

½   TEASPOON ONION POWDER

2   CELERY STALKS, CHOPPED

½   CUP CRUMBLED BLUE CHEESE

1   TEASPOON SALT

1   CUP PREPARED BUFFALO SAUCE

CHOPPED PARSLEY, FOR GARNISH (OPTIONAL)

Preheat the oven to 425 degrees F. Line a baking sheet with parchment paper.

In a large bowl, combine the ground chicken, breadcrumbs, egg, garlic powder, onion powder, celery, blue cheese, and salt. Gently mix until just combined; do not overmix, or your meatballs will be tough. Roll the chicken mixture into golf ball–sized meatballs. (You should have about 20.)

Place the meatballs on the parchment-lined baking sheet. Bake until browned and cooked through, about 10 to 12 minutes.

In a slow cooker, gently toss the meatballs with the Buffalo sauce, until the meatballs are covered in sauce. Cover and cook on low for 1½ hours, or until the sauce is warmed through. Garnish with chopped parsley if desired.

CRANBERRY TURKEY MEATBALLS

~

SERVES **8** • SLOW COOKER TIME **1 HOUR 30 MINUTES**

If you're hankering for a taste of Thanksgiving, try these turkey meatballs in a sweet-tangy cranberry chili sauce. You'll plump up the meatballs with onion, celery, and sage—ingredients you'd likely include in your holiday stuffing. Because you quickly bake the meatballs in the oven first, you don't need to worry about undercooking them in the slow cooker; you just need the sauce to warm through and for the ingredients to meld.

1   POUND GROUND TURKEY

¾   CUP PANKO BREADCRUMBS

1   LARGE EGG

½   CUP FINELY CHOPPED ONION

1   CELERY STALK, FINELY CHOPPED

1   TEASPOON DRIED SAGE

1   TEASPOON SALT

1   (14-OUNCE) CAN JELLIED CRANBERRY SAUCE

¾   CUP CHILI SAUCE

Preheat the oven to 425 degrees F. Line a baking sheet with parchment paper.

In a large bowl, combine the ground turkey, breadcrumbs, egg, onion, celery, sage, and salt. Gently mix until just combined; do not overmix, or your meatballs will be tough. Roll the turkey mixture into golf ball–sized meatballs. (You should have about 20.)

Place the meatballs on the parchment-lined baking sheet. Bake until browned and cooked through, about 10 to 12 minutes.

In a slow cooker, mix the cranberry sauce with the chili sauce. Add the meatballs and toss gently to coat with the sauce. Cover and cook on low for 1½ hours, or until the sauce is warmed through.

CHEESE-STUFFED MEATBALLS

～

SERVES 8 • SLOW COOKER TIME **5 HOURS 30 MINUTES**

When guests bite into these succulent meatballs, they'll find a delicious surprise inside—a warm, melty burst of mozzarella, which helps the meatballs stay juicy in the slow cooker. Make sure to cover the cheese with a good amount of meat mixture to get just the right ratio of meat-to-cheese.

1 (28-OUNCE) CAN CRUSHED TOMATOES

2 TABLESPOONS TOMATO PASTE

1 TEASPOON RED WINE VINEGAR

1 BASIL SPRIG, PLUS CHOPPED BASIL LEAVES FOR GARNISH

¼ TEASPOON CRUSHED RED PEPPER

4 GARLIC CLOVES, MINCED, DIVIDED

1 POUND GROUND BEEF

¾ CUP PANKO BREADCRUMBS

1 LARGE EGG

1 TEASPOON DRIED ROSEMARY

¼ CUP GRATED PARMESAN CHEESE

2 TEASPOONS SALT

½ TEASPOON FRESHLY GROUND BLACK PEPPER

8 OUNCES PART-SKIM LOW-MOISTURE MOZZARELLA, CUT INTO ¾-INCH CUBES (YOU SHOULD HAVE 20 TO 24 CUBES)

In a slow cooker, stir together the crushed tomatoes, tomato paste, vinegar, basil sprig, crushed red pepper, and half the garlic. Cover and cook on high for 4 hours.

Meanwhile, in a large bowl, combine the ground beef with the remaining garlic, the breadcrumbs, egg, rosemary, Parmesan, salt, and pepper. Gently mix until just combined; do not overmix, or your meatballs will be tough. Form portions of the meat mixture around the mozzarella cubes, making sure to cover the cheese completely. The meatballs should each be a little larger than a golf ball. (You should have 20 to 24.)

After the sauce has cooked for 4 hours, add the meatballs to the sauce, tossing gently to coat. Cover and cook on high for 1½ hours longer. Discard the basil sprig. Taste the sauce for seasoning and serve the meatballs garnished with additional chopped basil.

MEATBALL SLIDERS

~

SERVES **8** TO **10** • SLOW COOKER TIME **1 HOUR 30 MINUTES**

Juicy and hearty, these beef and pork meatballs are wonderful on their own and cook up beautifully in the slow cooker. Take them a step further by turning them into adorable little sliders—they're impossible to resist. The sliders are great with just the meatballs, sauce, and soft, squishy rolls, but you can jazz them up further by broiling the open-face meatball sandwiches topped with slices of provolone until melted, then topping with fresh basil leaves before serving.

1 POUND GROUND BEEF CHUCK

1 POUND GROUND PORK

½ CUP PANKO BREADCRUMBS

¼ CUP GRATED PARMESAN CHEESE

¼ CUP RICOTTA CHEESE

¼ CUP CHOPPED FRESH PARSLEY

2 LARGE EGGS

1 TABLESPOON SALT

1 RECIPE MARINARA DIPPING SAUCE (PAGE 19), OR 2 (24-OUNCE) JARS MARINARA SAUCE

24-30 DINNER POTATO ROLLS, SPLIT

In a large bowl, combine the ground beef, ground pork, breadcrumbs, Parmesan, ricotta, parsley, eggs, and salt. Gently mix until just combined; do not overmix, or your meatballs will be tough. Roll the meat mixture into golf ball–sized meatballs. (You should have about 24 to 30 meatballs).

In a slow cooker, add the marinara sauce. Place the meatballs in an even layer in the slow cooker, submerging them in the sauce as much as possible. Cover and cook on high for 1½ hours, or until the meatballs are cooked through.

To assemble the sliders, place 1 meatball on top of the bottom half of a potato roll. Top with some of the sauce and the other half of the roll.

SWEET AND STICKY CHICKEN WINGS

~

SERVES **8** TO **10** • SLOW COOKER TIME **3** TO **4 HOURS**

The sauce on these wings is spectacular—the fresh ginger adds a nice zing that cuts through the sweet, sticky honey and tangy balsamic vinegar. While it's an extra step, don't be tempted to skip broiling the wings after they're cooked; that's when the skin gets browned and slightly crisped. You can thicken the sauce on the stovetop while the wings are crisping up in the oven.

⅓ CUP SOY SAUCE

⅓ CUP BALSAMIC VINEGAR

¼ CUP BROWN SUGAR

¼ CUP HONEY

½ TEASPOON ONION POWDER

1 TEASPOON CAYENNE PEPPER

4 GARLIC CLOVES, MINCED

2 TABLESPOONS MINCED FRESH GINGER

1 TABLESPOON TABASCO SAUCE

4 POUNDS CHICKEN WINGS

1 TABLESPOON CORNSTARCH

In a slow cooker, whisk together the soy sauce, vinegar, brown sugar, honey, onion powder, cayenne, garlic, ginger, and Tabasco. Add the chicken wings and toss to coat with the sauce.

Cover and cook on low for 3 to 4 hours, or until the chicken wings are cooked through.

When the wings are almost done, preheat the oven to broil. Line a baking sheet with aluminum foil.

In a small bowl, whisk the cornstarch with 1 tablespoon of water.

When the wings are cooked, remove them from the slow cooker using tongs or a slotted spoon and place them on the foil-lined baking sheet. Broil until lightly caramelized, 6 to 7 minutes.

Meanwhile, pour the sauce from the slow cooker into a medium saucepan. Bring to a boil on the stovetop, whisk in the cornstarch mixture, reduce the heat, and let simmer rapidly until slightly thickened, about 5 minutes. Serve the wings with the sauce.

GLAZED COCKTAIL SAUSAGES

~

SERVES **8** TO **10** • SLOW COOKER TIME **2 HOURS**

When I was young, I used to adore Vienna sausages—those mini wieners of unidentifiable origin that came packed in pull-tab tin cans. I would heat them up on the stove and devour them plain. These little sausage snacks in a thick, tangy, flavor-packed sauce are definitely a big upgrade. The garlic adds a bit of a bite, while the hot sauce counteracts the sweet ketchup. To add a little color and some freshness, garnish with chopped parsley before serving.

¾ CUP KETCHUP

1 TABLESPOON DIJON MUSTARD

1 TABLESPOON WORCESTERSHIRE SAUCE

1 TABLESPOON SOY SAUCE

1 TABLESPOON HOT SAUCE

½ CUP BROWN SUGAR

4 GARLIC CLOVES, MINCED

2 (12-OUNCE) PACKAGES COCKTAIL SAUSAGES OR HOT DOGS, CUT INTO 2-INCH PIECES

CHOPPED PARSLEY, FOR GARNISH (OPTIONAL)

In a slow cooker, whisk together the ketchup, mustard, Worcestershire, soy sauce, hot sauce, brown sugar, and garlic. Add the sausages and toss to coat with the sauce.

Cover and cook on low for 2 hours. Garnish with chopped parsley if desired.

SPICY CHICKEN WINGS

~

SERVES **8** TO **10** • SLOW COOKER TIME **3** TO **4 HOURS**

If you're in the mood for something that's heavy on heat, these wings should do the trick. The type of hot sauce you use will determine the flavor of the final sauce, so choose wisely. (I like Melinda's Original Habanero Pepper Sauce, Extra Hot—highly recommended if you can handle a good amount of heat.)

½ CUP UNSALTED BUTTER, MELTED

3 TABLESPOONS SOY SAUCE

2 TABLESPOONS TOMATO PASTE

1 (5-OUNCE) BOTTLE HOT SAUCE

1 TABLESPOON DRIED OREGANO

1 TABLESPOON ONION POWDER

1 TABLESPOON GARLIC POWDER

4 POUNDS CHICKEN WINGS

1 TABLESPOON CORNSTARCH

¼ TEASPOON SALT

In a slow cooker, whisk together the melted butter, soy sauce, tomato paste, hot sauce, oregano, onion powder, and garlic powder. Add the chicken wings and toss to coat with the sauce.

Cover and cook on low for 3 to 4 hours, or until the chicken wings are cooked through.

When the wings are almost done, preheat the oven to broil. Line a baking sheet with aluminum foil.

In a small bowl, whisk the cornstarch with 1 tablespoon of water.

When the wings are cooked, remove them from the slow cooker using tongs or a slotted spoon and place them on the foil-lined baking sheet. Sprinkle with ¼ teaspoon salt. Broil until lightly caramelized, 6 to 7 minutes.

Meanwhile, pour the sauce from the slow cooker into a medium saucepan. Bring to a boil on the stovetop, whisk in the cornstarch mixture, reduce the heat, and let simmer rapidly until slightly thickened, about 5 minutes. Taste for seasoning. Serve the wings with the sauce.

BARBECUE RIBS

~

SERVES **6** • SLOW COOKER TIME **6 HOURS**

Tender, juicy ribs are a cinch to make in the slow cooker. Just season the meat with a chili rub, add some diced onions, and pour a homemade sauce over everything. Cook low and slow for a few hours, and you'll have delicious, fall-apart ribs in a sweet and tangy sauce that's perfect for feeding a crowd of meat lovers.

2 TEASPOONS CHILI POWDER

2 TEASPOONS GARLIC POWDER

2 TEASPOONS SALT

1 TEASPOON FRESHLY GROUND BLACK PEPPER

4 POUNDS BABY BACK RIBS, CUT INTO INDIVIDUAL RIBS

1 MEDIUM ONION, FINELY DICED

1 (15-OUNCE) CAN TOMATO SAUCE

1 (6-OUNCE) CAN TOMATO PASTE

2 TABLESPOONS CIDER VINEGAR

2 TABLESPOONS WORCESTERSHIRE SAUCE

2 TABLESPOONS SOY SAUCE

¼ CUP MOLASSES

In a small bowl, combine the chili powder, garlic powder, salt, and pepper. Mix well. Sprinkle the chili powder mixture over the ribs, then place the ribs in a slow cooker. Add the diced onion to the slow cooker, sprinkling evenly over the ribs.

In a medium bowl, mix the tomato sauce, tomato paste, vinegar, Worcestershire, soy sauce, and molasses. Pour the sauce evenly over the ribs.

Cover and cook on low for 6 hours, or until the ribs are tender. Toss the ribs in the sauce before serving.

WARM MARINATED MUSHROOMS

I'm not sure what it is about these mushrooms—the acidic bite of the white wine vinegar, the abundance of oregano and garlic, the meatiness of the mushrooms—but I can't stop eating them. Every time I cook a batch, I end up devouring a good portion of them in a single sitting . . . which doesn't leave much for my guests. They're also delicious served at room temperature or even cold. Try them yourself and see if they have the same effect on you!

2½ POUNDS CREMINI MUSHROOMS, CLEANED AND STEMS TRIMMED BUT NOT REMOVED

4 TABLESPOONS MINCED FRESH OREGANO

3 TABLESPOONS MINCED FRESH PARSLEY

3 GARLIC CLOVES, MINCED

2 TABLESPOONS WHITE WINE VINEGAR

2 TABLESPOONS OLIVE OIL

1 TEASPOON SALT

¼ TEASPOON FRESHLY GROUND BLACK PEPPER

1 TABLESPOON FRESH LEMON JUICE

Cut the mushrooms in half (you can quarter larger mushrooms; they should all be roughly the same size). Place them in the slow cooker. Add the oregano, parsley, garlic, vinegar, olive oil, salt, and pepper. Toss to combine.

Cover and cook on high for 2 to 3 hours, or until the mushrooms are tender. Stir in the lemon juice and taste for seasoning.

CRUNCHY PARTY MIX

~

SERVES 10 TO 12 • **SLOW COOKER TIME 3 HOURS**

This highly munchable snack—loaded with pretzels, nuts, bagel chips, and cereal—may resemble your typical party mix, but it isn't. Tabasco adds an unexpected little kick, and dried rosemary lends a surprisingly sophisticated touch. It's perfect for movie night or a TV binge-watching marathon.

3 CUPS CORN CHEX CEREAL

3 CUPS RICE CHEX CEREAL

3 CUPS WHEAT CHEX CEREAL

2 CUPS BROKEN BAGEL CHIPS

2 CUPS PRETZELS

½ CUP PEANUTS

½ CUP CASHEWS

1 TEASPOON GARLIC POWDER

1 TEASPOON ONION POWDER

1 TABLESPOON SALT

6 TABLESPOONS UNSALTED BUTTER, MELTED

4 TABLESPOONS WORCESTERSHIRE SAUCE

2 TABLESPOONS TABASCO SAUCE

2 TEASPOONS DRIED ROSEMARY

In a slow cooker, toss together the cereal, bagel chips, pretzels, peanuts, and cashews.

In a small bowl, whisk the garlic powder, onion powder, and salt with the melted butter until dissolved. Whisk in the Worcestershire, Tabasco, and rosemary. Pour the sauce over the cereal mixture and toss gently to coat.

Cover and cook on low for 3 hours, stirring every hour. Let cool in the slow cooker, uncovered. The mix can be stored in an airtight container at room temperature for up to a week.

GLAZED SPICED NUTS

~

MAKES **4 CUPS** • SLOW COOKER TIME **2 HOURS**

A little bit sweet, spicy, and citrusy, these nuts make a great party snack. I love the grated orange zest here— it adds a beautiful citrus note that balances out the rich maple syrup. I've used pecans, cashews, and peanuts, but feel free to change it up with your favorite nuts. The mixture can get a little sticky, so if you have a slow-cooker liner, you might want to use it here for easier cleanup.

½ CUP MAPLE SYRUP

3 TABLESPOONS UNSALTED BUTTER, MELTED

2 TEASPOONS GROUND CINNAMON

2 TEASPOONS FINELY GRATED ORANGE ZEST

1 TEASPOON CAYENNE PEPPER

1 TEASPOON SALT

2 CUPS PECANS

1 CUP CASHEWS

1 CUP PEANUTS

Spray the inside of a slow cooker with cooking spray, or line with a liner and spray with cooking spray.

In a large bowl, whisk together the maple syrup, melted butter, cinnamon, orange zest, cayenne, and salt. Add the pecans, cashews, and peanuts and toss to coat.

Place the nuts in the slow cooker in an even layer. Cover and cook on high for 1 hour.

Stir the nuts and continue to cook on high, uncovered, for 1 hour, stirring occasionally.

Line a baking sheet with parchment paper. Pour the nuts onto the parchment-lined baking sheet and spread out. Let cool completely. The nuts can be stored in an airtight container for up to a week.

CINNAMON-SUGAR ALMONDS

~

MAKES **3 CUPS** • SLOW COOKER TIME **3 HOURS**

This recipe produces deliciously cinnamony, sugary, sticky-crunchy almonds. It's not completely set-it-and-forget-it—there's some intermittent stirring that takes only a few seconds and is essential to prevent the nuts from clumping together. While I don't usually cook with slow cooker liners, I would recommend using one here. And if you know your slow cooker tends to cook on the high side, I would recommend cooking the almonds entirely on low.

¾ CUP WHITE SUGAR

¾ CUP BROWN SUGAR

3 TABLESPOONS GROUND CINNAMON

¼ TEASPOON SALT

1 EGG WHITE

2 TEASPOONS VANILLA EXTRACT

3 CUPS ALMONDS

Spray the inside of a slow cooker with cooking spray, or line with a liner and spray with cooking spray.

In a gallon-size resealable plastic bag, combine the white sugar, brown sugar, cinnamon, and salt. Set aside.

In a small bowl, whisk together the egg white and the vanilla until the mixture becomes foamy. Add the almonds and toss to completely coat the almonds with the egg white mixture.

Add the almonds to the bag with the cinnamon sugar, seal securely, and toss until the almonds are completely coated. Evenly spread the almonds in the slow cooker.

Cover and cook on high for 2 hours (or on low for 4 hours, if you're worried about scorching), stirring every 30 minutes. After 2 hours, uncover and pour ⅛ cup water over the almonds. Reduce the heat to low and cook for 1 more hour, stirring after 30 minutes.

Line a baking sheet with parchment paper. Pour the almonds onto the sheet and let cool. Store in an airtight container for up to a week.

CHAPTER 3

SIDE DISHES

GARLIC MASHED POTATOES

~

SERVES 8 TO 10 • SLOW COOKER TIME 4 HOURS

The best thing about making mashed potatoes in the slow cooker? You can serve them warm directly out of the appliance and avoid having a bowl of cold, gluey potatoes congealing on the table. If you like a more rustic look, feel free to leave the potatoes unpeeled.

4 POUNDS YUKON GOLD POTATOES, PEELED AND CUBED

8 GARLIC CLOVES, MINCED

2½ TEASPOONS SALT

½ TEASPOON FRESHLY GROUND BLACK PEPPER

6 TABLESPOONS UNSALTED BUTTER, MELTED

1 CUP WHOLE MILK

¾ CUP HEAVY CREAM

In a slow cooker, toss the potatoes with the garlic, salt, and pepper. Cover and cook on high for 4 hours, or until the potatoes are tender.

Mash the potatoes directly in the slow cooker with a potato masher or wooden spoon. Mash in the butter, milk, and cream and allow to warm through. Taste for seasoning.

SWEET POTATO MASH

~

SERVES **8** TO **10** • SLOW COOKER TIME **3** TO **4** HOURS

Skip the marshmallows and the loads of sugar. Sweet potatoes don't need much to make them delicious—just a touch of brown sugar, spices, butter, and cream. Some fresh orange juice adds a nice citrus brightness and allows the sweet, nutty potatoes to shine through.

6 SWEET POTATOES, PEELED AND CUBED

½ CUP FRESH ORANGE JUICE

1 TABLESPOON BROWN SUGAR

1 TEASPOON GROUND CINNAMON

½ TEASPOON GROUND NUTMEG

1 TEASPOON SALT

4 TABLESPOONS UNSALTED BUTTER, MELTED

3 TABLESPOONS HEAVY CREAM

In a slow cooker, place the sweet potatoes in an even layer.

In a medium bowl, whisk together the orange juice, brown sugar, cinnamon, nutmeg, and salt. Pour the mixture over the sweet potatoes.

Cover and cook on high for 3 to 4 hours, or until the potatoes are tender. Mash the potatoes directly in the slow cooker with a potato masher or wooden spoon. Stir in the butter and cream and allow to warm through. Taste for seasoning.

CHEESY BACON POTATOES

~

SERVES **6 TO 8** • SLOW COOKER TIME **3 HOURS**

Think plain mashed potatoes are a little too basic? If you love loaded baked potatoes, you'll adore this decadent side that's chock-full of familiar ingredients: sour cream, cheese, scallions, and bacon.

2 POUNDS RUSSET POTATOES, PEELED AND CUBED

2 CUPS SOUR CREAM

2 CUPS SHREDDED CHEDDAR CHEESE

6 SCALLIONS, SLICED, PLUS MORE FOR GARNISH

6 SLICES BACON, COOKED AND CHOPPED

In a slow cooker, place the potatoes in an even layer. Cover and cook on high for 2 hours, or until the potatoes are tender.

Mash the potatoes directly in the slow cooker with a potato masher or wooden spoon. Stir in the sour cream, cheddar, scallions, and bacon. Cover and cook on low for 1 hour, or until the cheese has melted.

Stir thoroughly, making sure all the ingredients are well-combined. Garnish with the additional scallions and serve.

CREAMY CORN CASSEROLE

~

SERVES 8 • **SLOW COOKER TIME 3 HOURS 30 MINUTES TO 4 HOURS**

Corn is one of my favorite vegetables, so I'm a huge fan of this creamy, homey side. The corn cooks with cream cheese, cheddar, and some flour and cornmeal to give the dish a little more structure. It's a decadent side dish that will really stand out on your holiday table.

8 OUNCES CREAM CHEESE, SOFTENED

1 TABLESPOON SUGAR

2 LARGE EGGS

½ CUP ALL-PURPOSE FLOUR

¼ CUP CORNMEAL

1 TEASPOON BAKING POWDER

1 TEASPOON SALT

¼ TEASPOON FRESHLY GROUND BLACK PEPPER

½ TEASPOON CAYENNE

2 TABLESPOONS UNSALTED BUTTER, MELTED

1½ CUPS WHOLE MILK

½ CUP HEAVY CREAM

1 JALAPEÑO PEPPER, SEEDED AND MINCED

2 CUPS SHREDDED CHEDDAR CHEESE

4 CUPS CORN, FRESH OR FROZEN AND THAWED

Spray the inside of a slow cooker with cooking spray.

In a large bowl, beat the cream cheese with the sugar until fluffy using an electric mixer. Beat in the eggs one at a time. Stir in the flour, cornmeal, baking powder, salt, pepper, and cayenne, mixing thoroughly. Add the butter, milk, and cream, mixing thoroughly. Stir in the jalapeño, cheddar, and corn, making sure everything is combined.

Pour the mixture into the slow cooker. Cover and cook on low for 3½ to 4 hours, until the casserole is puffy and set on top.

SOUTHERN GREEN BEANS

~

SERVES **8** • SLOW COOKER TIME **8 HOURS**

These slow-cooked, melt-in-your mouth green beans have a nice tang, thanks to a healthy dose of white wine vinegar. Diced ham adds salty, porky goodness and makes this a hearty side dish.

2 POUNDS GREEN BEANS, TRIMMED AND CUT INTO 2-INCH PIECES

1 CUP DICED RED ONION

1 CUP DICED COOKED HAM

2 CUPS CHICKEN BROTH

2 TABLESPOONS WHITE WINE VINEGAR, PLUS MORE AS NEEDED

½ CUP TOMATO SAUCE

5 GARLIC CLOVES, MINCED

1 TEASPOON CAYENNE PEPPER

1 TEASPOON SALT

In a slow cooker, stir together the green beans, onion, ham, broth, vinegar, tomato sauce, garlic, cayenne, and salt.

Cover and cook on low for 8 hours or until the beans are tender. Taste for seasoning and add more vinegar if needed.

BROWN SUGAR CARROTS

~

SERVES **6** TO **8** • SLOW COOKER TIME **4** TO **5** HOURS

I usually prefer raw carrots over cooked, but I'll happily indulge in this simple side dish anytime. Sweet and buttery, the carrots cook to tender perfection in the slow cooker. Chopped parsley adds a fresh herbal note and makes the carrots look extra pretty for the dinner table.

3 POUNDS CARROTS, PEELED AND SLICED ¼-INCH THICK

1½ TEASPOONS SALT

¼ CUP BROWN SUGAR

3 TABLESPOONS UNSALTED BUTTER, CUT INTO PIECES

CHOPPED FRESH PARSLEY, FOR GARNISH (OPTIONAL)

In a slow cooker, place the carrots in an even layer. Sprinkle with the salt, sugar, and butter.

Cover and cook on low for 4 to 5 hours, or until the carrots are tender. Stir the carrots and sprinkle with chopped parsley before serving if desired.

MOLASSES BAKED BEANS

~

SERVES **8** • SLOW COOKER TIME **9** TO **10 HOURS**

Cooking dried beans in the slow cooker is a fantastic technique, because you can skip soaking them overnight. These "baked" beans simmer with bacon, brown sugar, molasses, and mustard, resulting in an intensely flavorful side dish.

1 POUND DRIED NAVY BEANS, SORTED AND RINSED

1 YELLOW ONION, MINCED

½ POUND BACON, COOKED AND CHOPPED INTO 1-INCH PIECES

¼ CUP BROWN SUGAR

¼ CUP MOLASSES

1 TABLESPOON TOMATO PASTE

1 TEASPOON MUSTARD POWDER

1 TEASPOON SALT

¼ TEASPOON FRESHLY GROUND BLACK PEPPER

4 TEASPOONS CIDER VINEGAR

In a slow cooker, stir together the beans, onion, bacon, brown sugar, molasses, tomato paste, mustard powder, salt, pepper, and 4½ cups water.

Cover and cook on low for 9 to 10 hours, or until the beans are tender. Stir in the cider vinegar and taste for seasoning.

CORNBREAD STUFFING

~

SERVES **8** TO **10** • SLOW COOKER TIME **5 HOURS**

You can use store-bought cornbread in this recipe, or bake your own. Don't worry if the cornbread cubes start to break up when you toss together the ingredients; it's inevitable. The sweetness of the cornbread pairs nicely with the meaty mushrooms and savory poultry seasoning.

10 CUPS CORNBREAD, CUT INTO 1-INCH CUBES

2 CUPS DICED CELERY

1 YELLOW ONION, DICED

1 POUND CREMINI MUSHROOMS, SLICED

¼ CUP UNSALTED BUTTER, MELTED

2 TABLESPOONS POULTRY SEASONING

2 TEASPOONS SALT

½ TEASPOON FRESHLY GROUND BLACK PEPPER

2 LARGE EGGS, BEATEN

3 CUPS CHICKEN OR VEGETABLE BROTH

Spray the inside of a slow cooker with cooking spray.

In a very large bowl, toss together the cornbread, celery, onion, mushrooms, butter, poultry seasoning, salt, and pepper. Gently mix in the eggs. Place the mixture in the slow cooker.

Pour the broth over the cornbread mixture and stir gently to combine. Cover and cook on low for 5 hours, or until the vegetables are tender. Taste for seasoning.

WILTED COLLARD GREENS

~

SERVES **10** TO **12** • SLOW COOKER TIME **6** TO **7** HOURS

I'm obsessed with leafy greens; I can eat amazingly large quantities of cooked greens in one sitting. So it's a good thing this recipe makes a lot! Your slow cooker will start out overflowing with collards, but don't worry—they'll gradually wilt down as they cook. If you can't find ham hocks, smoked turkey drumsticks or smoked ham will also work in this recipe. The cider vinegar provides an essential dash of acid; feel free to add more before serving, if needed.

3 BUNCHES COLLARD GREENS

1 POUND SMOKED HAM HOCKS OR SMOKED TURKEY DRUMSTICKS, OR ½ POUND DICED SMOKED HAM

1 YELLOW ONION, DICED

5 GARLIC CLOVES, MINCED

1 TABLESPOON SUGAR

2 TEASPOONS SALT

½ TEASPOON FRESHLY GROUND BLACK PEPPER

2 TABLESPOONS CIDER VINEGAR, PLUS MORE AS NEEDED

1 TABLESPOON TABASCO SAUCE

4 CUPS CHICKEN BROTH

Using your hands or a sharp knife, strip the collard leaves from the tough stems. Discard the stems. Tear or cut the collard leaves into bite-size pieces.

Place the ham hocks, turkey drumsticks, or cooked ham in a slow cooker. Add the onion, garlic, and collard greens (don't worry if it seems like you have too many greens; they'll cook down). Sprinkle with the sugar, salt, and black pepper. Add the vinegar, Tabasco, and chicken broth to the slow cooker.

Cover and cook on low for 6 to 7 hours, or until the greens are very tender. If using, transfer the ham hocks or drumsticks to a cutting board and remove the meat from the bones. Discard the skin and bones; shred the meat, then return it to the slow cooker and stir it into the greens. Taste for seasoning and add more salt, pepper, and vinegar as needed.

SAUSAGE AND SAGE STUFFING

~

SERVES **8 TO 10** • SLOW COOKER TIME **4 TO 5 HOURS**

Cooking Thanksgiving stuffing in a slow cooker frees up a lot of space when you're trying to deal with the bird, the sweet potato casserole, and a whole host of other dishes. Since I'm a bit lazy, I love that you don't need to sauté the sausage separately before making the stuffing—the raw sausage cooks in the slow cooker along with the rest of the ingredients. If you want a spicier stuffing, feel free to swap in hot Italian sausage instead of sweet.

1½ BAGUETTES, CUT INTO 1-INCH PIECES (ABOUT 10 CUPS)

1 YELLOW ONION, DICED

3 CARROTS, PEELED AND DICED

3 CELERY STALKS, DICED

1 TABLESPOON DRIED SAGE

1 STICK UNSALTED BUTTER, CUT INTO PIECES

1 TEASPOON SALT

½ TEASPOON FRESHLY GROUND PEPPER

1½ CUPS CHICKEN BROTH

1 POUND SWEET ITALIAN SAUSAGE, CASINGS REMOVED

Spray the inside of a slow cooker with cooking spray.

In a very large bowl, toss together the bread, onion, carrots, celery, sage, butter, salt, and pepper. Place the mixture in the slow cooker.

Pour the chicken broth over the bread mixture. Using your hands, break the sausage into teaspoon-size pieces and scatter evenly over the bread mixture.

Cover and cook on low for 4 to 5 hours, or until the sausage is cooked and the vegetables are tender. Gently toss the ingredients to combine and then taste for seasoning.

CHEESY SUMMER SQUASH CASSEROLE

~

SERVES **6** TO **8** • SLOW COOKER TIME **4** TO **5 HOURS**

If you cover anything in melted cheese, it has to be good, right? I've seen many squash casserole recipes that call for tons of cheese and cream, but this one is much lighter. There's just enough mozzarella to add a little lusciousness, but the tender, delicate squash remains the star. If you want to take it a step further, transfer the squash when it's cooked to an ovenproof casserole dish and broil for a few minutes, until the top is bubbly and browned.

1½ POUNDS ZUCCHINI, CUT INTO ¼-INCH-THICK SLICES

1½ POUNDS YELLOW SQUASH, CUT INTO ¼-INCH-THICK SLICES

3 GARLIC CLOVES, MINCED

1 TEASPOON SALT

¼ TEASPOON FRESHLY GROUND BLACK PEPPER

1 TEASPOON ITALIAN SEASONING

¼ CUP UNSALTED BUTTER, CUT INTO SMALL PIECES

¼ CUP GRATED PARMESAN CHEESE

¼ CUP PLAIN BREADCRUMBS

1 CUP SHREDDED MOZZARELLA

In a slow cooker, combine the zucchini, yellow squash, and garlic. Toss with the salt, pepper, and Italian seasoning. Sprinkle with the butter, Parmesan, breadcrumbs, and mozzarella.

Cover and cook on low for 4 to 5 hours, or until the cheese has melted and the squash is tender.

RED BEANS AND RICE

~

SERVES **10** TO **12** AS A SIDE; **8** TO **10** AS A MAIN
SLOW COOKER TIME **9** TO **10** HOURS

You can serve this traditional Louisiana dish as a hearty side or a vegetarian main (use vegetable broth instead of chicken if you're going the veggie route). Make sure to use instant rice—also known as minute rice—in this recipe for tender, fluffy results; I've found that other types of rice don't turn out properly in the slow cooker. (Believe me, I've tried!)

1   POUND DRIED KIDNEY BEANS, SORTED AND RINSED

2   GREEN BELL PEPPERS, DICED

1   YELLOW ONION, DICED

2   CELERY STALKS, DICED

3   GARLIC CLOVES, MINCED

2   BAY LEAVES

3   TABLESPOONS CAJUN SEASONING

1   TABLESPOON SALT

½   TEASPOON FRESHLY GROUND BLACK PEPPER

4   CUPS CHICKEN OR VEGETABLE BROTH

1   CUP INSTANT WHITE RICE

2   TABLESPOONS RED WINE VINEGAR

3   SCALLIONS, SLICED

In a slow cooker, stir together the beans, bell peppers, onion, celery, garlic, and bay leaves. Add the Cajun seasoning, salt, black pepper, broth, and 3 cups water; stir to combine.

Cover and cook on low for 9 to 10 hours, or until the beans and vegetables are tender. Stir in the rice; cover and cook on high for 1 hour. Stir in the vinegar and taste for seasoning. Sprinkle with the scallions and serve.

EASY DINNER ROLLS

~

MAKES **8 ROLLS** • SLOW COOKER TIME **1 HOUR**

Bread in the slow cooker? Absolutely! It's amazing how easily this no-knead recipe comes together. And with just four ingredients, it's simple, too. Don't forget to brush the cooked rolls with plenty of melted butter before serving; they really benefit from the extra flavor boost. The rolls will inevitably stick together as they cook so they won't be as perfectly shaped as rolls baked in the oven, but they'll still taste great.

1 (¼-OUNCE) PACKET ACTIVE DRY YEAST

2¼ TEASPOONS SALT

3 CUPS ALL-PURPOSE FLOUR

MELTED UNSALTED BUTTER, FOR BRUSHING

In a large bowl, combine 1½ cups warm water (the water should be between 95 and 115 degrees F) with the yeast and salt. Stir. Add the flour and stir to combine, making sure all the flour is incorporated. Cover the bowl with plastic wrap, place in a warm spot, and let rise until doubled in size, about 1 hour.

Line a slow cooker with parchment paper. Punch down the dough, then divide it into 8 equal portions using a knife or bench scraper. Roll each piece of dough into a ball and place in the slow cooker, spacing evenly.

Cover and cook on high for 1 hour, or until the rolls are cooked through. Brush the tops of the rolls with melted butter and serve.

CHAPTER 4

MAIN DISHES

BROWN SUGAR CIDER HAM

~

SERVES **8** TO **10** • SLOW COOKER TIME **4** TO **5** HOURS

A whole holiday ham is a wondrous thing. Why not make it even more fantastic with apple cider, maple syrup (use the real thing, please!), brown sugar, and Dijon mustard? Buy a spiral-cut ham to make carving easier, and make sure to remove the cloves before serving.

¼ CUP BROWN SUGAR

1 (7-POUND) BONE-IN, SPIRAL-CUT HAM

1 TABLESPOON WHOLE CLOVES

1½ CUPS APPLE CIDER

¼ CUP MAPLE SYRUP

2 TABLESPOONS DIJON MUSTARD

¼ TEASPOON FRESHLY GROUND BLACK PEPPER

Rub the brown sugar all over the ham, then place the meat in a slow cooker. Stud the ham with cloves.

In a medium bowl, whisk together the cider, maple syrup, mustard, and pepper. Pour the cider mixture over the ham.

Cover and cook on low for 4 to 5 hours, basting occasionally. Remove the cloves before serving.

HERBED TURKEY BREAST

~

SERVES 8 TO 10 • SLOW COOKER TIME 6 TO 7 HOURS

Cooking a turkey in the slow cooker guarantees juicy, flavorful results every time. Unfortunately, however, you won't get a nice crisp skin solely in the slow cooker. You'll need to broil the bird in the oven for a couple minutes to brown up the skin (don't broil for too long, or the meat will start to dry out).

1 CARROT, PEELED AND CHOPPED INTO 1-INCH PIECES

1 ONION, CHOPPED INTO 1-INCH PIECES

1 CELERY STALK, CHOPPED INTO 1-INCH PIECES

3 TABLESPOONS ONION POWDER

½ TEASPOON DRIED SAGE

½ TEASPOON CELERY SEED

1 TEASPOON DRIED PARSLEY

1 TEASPOON SALT

½ TEASPOON FRESHLY GROUND BLACK PEPPER

1 (6- TO 7-POUND) BONE-IN TURKEY BREAST

2 TABLESPOONS UNSALTED BUTTER, MELTED

2 TABLESPOONS CORNSTARCH

In a slow cooker, toss together the carrot, onion, and celery.

In a small bowl, mix herbs and spices.

Place the turkey in the slow cooker on top of the vegetables. Sprinkle with the spice mixture and drizzle with the melted butter.

Cover and cook on low for 6 to 7 hours, or until the turkey is fully cooked (165 degrees F).

When the turkey is almost done, preheat the oven to broil. In a small bowl, whisk the cornstarch with 2 tablespoons water.

When the turkey is cooked, transfer it to a roasting pan with a rack. Broil until the skin begins to crisp, about 2 minutes.

Meanwhile, strain the remaining liquid in the slow cooker into a saucepan. Bring to a boil over medium-high heat. Whisk in the cornstarch mixture and cook until the gravy thickens, about 5 minutes. Slice the turkey and serve with the gravy.

BRISKET AND ONIONS

~

SERVES **6** TO **8** • SLOW COOKER TIME **8** TO **9** HOURS

While I try to keep slow cooker meals as simple as possible, in this case, I think it's important to cook the onions and sear the brisket in advance. You'll develop much better flavor and the end results are well worth it.

2 TABLESPOONS CANOLA OR VEGETABLE OIL, DIVIDED

2 LARGE YELLOW ONIONS, SLICED INTO HALF MOONS

1 (4-POUND) BEEF BRISKET

1½ TABLESPOONS SALT

2 TEASPOONS FRESHLY GROUND BLACK PEPPER

2 CUPS BEEF BROTH

2 TABLESPOONS WORCESTERSHIRE SAUCE

1 TABLESPOON SOY SAUCE

1 TABLESPOON TOMATO PASTE

1 TABLESPOON RED WINE VINEGAR

6 GARLIC CLOVES, MINCED

In a large skillet, heat 1 tablespoon oil over medium heat. Add the onions and cook, stirring occasionally, until tender and browned, about 20 minutes.

Meanwhile, pat the brisket dry and season all over with the salt and pepper. In a second large skillet, heat the remaining 1 tablespoon oil over medium-high heat. Add the brisket and cook until both sides are browned, about 10 minutes. Remove and place in a slow cooker.

In a large bowl, whisk together the broth, Worcestershire, soy sauce, tomato paste, and red wine vinegar.

Sprinkle the garlic and caramelized onions over the meat. Pour the broth mixture into the slow cooker. Cover and cook on low for 8 to 9 hours, until the brisket is very tender. Slice or shred the brisket and serve with the onions and juices.

MAIN DISHES

67

HEARTY BEEF STEW WITH CARROTS AND PEAS

~

SERVES **8** TO **10** • SLOW COOKER TIME **8 HOURS**

A robust, full-bodied beef stew is one of my ultimate comfort foods, so a classic boeuf bourguignon always hits the spot. While nothing compares to Julia Child's original recipe, this pared-down slow cooker riff is tasty in its own right. My version includes soy sauce, which sounds strange, but it helps round out the savory, beefy flavor. I like to dredge the meat in flour and brown it first to add more depth to the dish, as well as help thicken up the sauce. Stirring in peas at the end retains their bright color, which makes each bowl of stew especially lovely.

4 POUNDS BEEF CHUCK, TRIMMED OF FAT AND CUT INTO 1-INCH PIECES

½ CUP ALL-PURPOSE FLOUR

2 TABLESPOONS OLIVE OIL

½ CUP DRY RED WINE

2 YELLOW ONIONS, DICED

2 RED POTATOES, CUT INTO 2-INCH PIECES

½ POUND CARROTS, PEELED AND CUT INTO 1-INCH PIECES

6 GARLIC CLOVES, MINCED

1 (6-OUNCE) CAN TOMATO PASTE

2 CUPS BEEF BROTH

¼ CUP SOY SAUCE

1 BAY LEAF

1 TEASPOON DRIED THYME

1 TABLESPOON SALT

1 CUP FROZEN PEAS

In a large bowl, toss the beef in the flour, shaking off any excess.

In a large skillet, heat the oil over medium-high heat. Add a few pieces of beef and cook until browned on all sides, about 6 to 8 minutes. Remove with a slotted spoon to a slow cooker. Repeat with the remaining beef and continue browning in batches until all the meat is in the slow cooker.

Add the wine to the skillet, scraping up any browned bits. Pour the wine into the slow cooker. Stir in the onions, potatoes, carrots, garlic, tomato paste, broth, soy sauce, bay leaf, thyme, and salt.

Cover and cook on low for 8 hours, until the beef and vegetables are tender. Stir in the peas and allow to warm through. Taste for seasoning.

POT ROAST WITH VEGETABLES

SERVES **6** TO **8** • SLOW COOKER TIME **9 HOURS**

Tender, meaty pot roast served with a medley of vegetables and rich gravy—it doesn't get any better than this. Seasoned with black pepper, thyme, rosemary, paprika, and garlic, the beef has loads of flavor. Serve it on a platter with the vegetables for a company-worthy feast.

1 POUND CARROTS, PEELED AND CUT INTO 2-INCH PIECES

2 POUNDS RED POTATOES, CUT INTO 2-INCH PIECES

1 YELLOW ONION, CUT INTO 2-INCH PIECES

2 STALKS CELERY, CUT INTO 2-INCH PIECES

1 TEASPOON DRIED THYME

1 TEASPOON DRIED ROSEMARY

1 TEASPOON PAPRIKA

1 TEASPOON GARLIC POWDER

1½ TABLESPOONS SALT

2 TEASPOONS FRESHLY GROUND BLACK PEPPER

1 (4-POUND) CHUCK ROAST

1 CUP BEEF BROTH

1 TABLESPOON CORNSTARCH

In a slow cooker, toss together the carrots, potatoes, onion, and celery.

In a small bowl, mix together the thyme, rosemary, paprika, garlic powder, salt, and pepper. Pat the roast dry and rub all over with the spice mixture. Place the pot roast on top of the vegetables in the slow cooker.

Pour the broth over the roast. Cover and cook on low for 9 hours, or until the beef and vegetables are tender.

In a small bowl, whisk the cornstarch with 1 tablespoon water.

Transfer the beef and vegetables to a platter and pour the cooking liquid into a saucepan. Bring the liquid to a boil on the stovetop. Whisk in the cornstarch mixture, reduce the heat, and let simmer rapidly until the gravy thickens, about 5 minutes. Taste for seasoning and serve with the pot roast and vegetables.

CHICKEN AND SAUSAGE GUMBO

~

SERVES **8** • SLOW COOKER TIME **4 HOURS**

A classic Louisiana stew, gumbo makes a soul-satisfying one-bowl meal. Use andouille sausage—a slightly smoky, spicy sausage that's a hallmark of Creole cuisine—to give it authentic flair. Sliced okra helps thicken the stew, along with a little cornstarch. It's traditionally served over white rice; I like it just fine on its own, too.

1½ POUNDS BONELESS, SKIN-LESS CHICKEN THIGHS, CUT INTO 1½-INCH PIECES

¾ POUND ANDOUILLE SAU-SAGE, SLICED ½-INCH THICK

½ POUND OKRA, SLICED CROSSWISE ½-INCH THICK

1 GREEN BELL PEPPER, CHOPPED

3 CELERY STALKS, CHOPPED

1 YELLOW ONION, CHOPPED

½ TEASPOON CAYENNE PEPPER

½ TEASPOON SALT

1 (14.5-OUNCE) CAN DICED TOMATOES

2 CUPS CHICKEN BROTH

¼ CUP CORNSTARCH

SLICED SCALLIONS, FOR GARNISH

WHITE RICE, FOR SERVING (OPTIONAL)

In a slow cooker, combine the chicken, sausage, okra, bell pepper, celery, onion, cayenne pepper, and salt. Stir in the diced tomatoes with their juices and chicken broth. Cover and cook on high for 3 hours.

In a small bowl, whisk together the cornstarch with ¼ cup water. Stir into the gumbo to thicken it. Cover and cook for 1 hour, or until the chicken is cooked through and the vegetables are tender. Taste for seasoning. Serve garnished with sliced scallions over white rice, if desired.

SPICY MEXICAN CHICKEN STEW

~

SERVES **6** TO **8** • SLOW COOKER TIME **4 HOURS**

This festive meal is anything but boring; it's bursting with shredded chicken, corn, and includes a jar of store-bought salsa (an effective shortcut). I recommend choosing a spicy one to give the stew a lively kick.

1 (16-OUNCE) JAR SPICY SALSA

1½ TEASPOONS GROUND CUMIN

1 TEASPOON CHILI POWDER

2 TEASPOONS SALT

½ TEASPOON FRESHLY GROUND BLACK PEPPER

1½ POUNDS RUSSET POTATOES, PEELED AND DICED INTO 1-INCH CUBES

1 (16-OUNCE) PACKAGE FROZEN CORN

2 CELERY STALKS, CUT INTO 1-INCH PIECES

2 CARROTS, PEELED AND CUT INTO 1-INCH PIECES

1 ONION, DICED

2 GARLIC CLOVES, MINCED

6 BONELESS, SKINLESS CHICKEN THIGHS

1½ CUPS CHICKEN BROTH

In a slow cooker, stir together the salsa, cumin, chili powder, salt, and pepper. Add the potatoes, corn, celery, carrots, onion, and garlic, tossing to coat. Place the chicken on top of the vegetables and pour the broth into the slow cooker.

Cover and cook on high for 4 hours, or until the chicken is cooked through and the vegetables are tender. Using two forks, shred the chicken and stir it into the liquid. Taste for seasoning.

OLD-FASHIONED
CHICKEN AND BISCUITS

~

SERVES **6** • SLOW COOKER TIME **6** TO **7 HOURS**

Chicken and biscuits is one of my all-time favorite meals. There's something I find incredibly comforting about the combination of chicken, tender veggies, creamy broth, and buttery biscuit; it's like a chicken pot pie, but even better. These "biscuits" are more of a cross between something you'd bake in the oven and a lighter dumpling that steams on top of a chicken stew. Making this meal in a slow cooker is especially fun because the biscuits cook right on top of the chicken and broth.

FOR THE STEW:

- **4** CARROTS, PEELED AND DICED

- **3** STALKS CELERY, DICED

- **1** YELLOW ONION, DICED

- ¼ CUP ALL-PURPOSE FLOUR

- 1½ POUNDS BONELESS, SKINLESS CHICKEN THIGHS, CUT INTO BITE-SIZE PIECES

- **1** TABLESPOON POULTRY SEASONING

- **1** TEASPOON SALT

- 1½ CUPS CHICKEN BROTH

- **1** CUP FROZEN PEAS

- ½ CUP HEAVY CREAM

To make the stew: In a slow cooker, toss the carrots, celery, and onion with the flour. Place the chicken on top of the vegetables and sprinkle with the poultry seasoning and salt. Pour the chicken broth over the chicken and vegetables.

Cover and cook on low for 5 to 6 hours, or until the chicken and vegetables are tender.

Make the biscuits shortly before the stew is done: In a large bowl, whisk together the flour, salt, and baking powder. Whisk in the butter, then the milk. Set aside.

FOR THE BISCUITS:

1 CUP ALL-PURPOSE FLOUR

½ TEASPOON SALT

1½ TEASPOONS BAKING POWDER

2 TABLESPOONS UNSALTED BUTTER, MELTED

½ CUP WHOLE MILK

After 5 to 6 hours of stew-cooking time, stir the frozen peas and heavy cream into the chicken stew. Drop heaping tablespoons of the biscuit batter on top of the chicken mixture, spacing them evenly. Cover and cook on high for 1 hour, or until the biscuits have puffed up and are cooked through.

Serve the chicken stew in bowls topped with the biscuits.

CORNED BEEF AND CABBAGE

～

SERVES **6** TO **8** • SLOW COOKER TIME **7** TO **8** HOURS

I originally wanted to include a whole head of cabbage in this recipe—I'm always a fan of adding more vegetables—but I quickly realized that it's physically impossible for a 6-quart slow cooker to contain that much cabbage along with the other ingredients. Don't worry, half a cabbage is plenty! The mild veggies are the perfect foil for the salty, seasoned corned beef; serve with tangy mustard on the side.

1 POUND CARROTS, PEELED AND CUT INTO 1-INCH PIECES

1 POUND RED POTATOES, QUARTERED (OR CUT INTO EIGHTHS IF THE POTATOES ARE LARGE)

½ GREEN CABBAGE, CUT INTO THIN SLICES

6 FRESH THYME SPRIGS

1 (4-POUND) CORNED BEEF BRISKET WITH SPICE PACKET

DIJON MUSTARD, FOR SERVING

In a slow cooker, combine the carrots, potatoes, cabbage, thyme, spice packet contents, and ½ cup water. Place the beef on top of the vegetables.

Cover and cook on low for 7 to 8 hours, or until the beef and vegetables are tender. Thinly slice the beef and serve with the vegetables and mustard.

MAIN DISHES

77

SMOKY BEEF CHILI

~

SERVES **6 TO 8** • SLOW COOKER TIME **7 HOURS**

On a chilly (no pun intended) winter day, there's nothing better than a rib-sticking bowl of chili. The chipotles really make this dish stand out, adding a lovely smokiness and a hint of spice. Cut-up pieces of beef chuck hold their shape and texture in this chili, making it a better choice than ground beef.

1½ POUNDS BEEF CHUCK, CUT INTO ¾-INCH PIECES

3 (15.5-OUNCE) CANS KIDNEY BEANS, RINSED AND DRAINED

1 YELLOW ONION, CHOPPED

4 GARLIC CLOVES, CHOPPED

1 (28-OUNCE) CAN DICED TOMATOES

¼ CUP TOMATO PASTE

1 CUP TOMATO PURÉE

3 TEASPOONS CHOPPED CHIPOTLE CHILES IN ADOBO SAUCE, PLUS 1 TEASPOON SAUCE

2 TABLESPOONS SOY SAUCE

2 TABLESPOONS ALL-PURPOSE FLOUR

3 TABLESPOONS CHILI POWDER

1 TABLESPOON GROUND CUMIN

½ TEASPOON SALT

GRATED CHEDDAR CHEESE, SOUR CREAM, CHOPPED RED ONION, AND CHOPPED CILANTRO, FOR SERVING

In a slow cooker, stir together the beef, beans, onion, garlic, diced tomatoes and their juices, tomato paste, tomato purée, chipotles and adobo sauce, soy sauce, flour, chili powder, cumin, and salt.

Cover and cook on low for 7 hours, or until the beef and vegetables are tender. Taste for seasoning and serve with the cheddar, sour cream, red onion, and cilantro.

MAIN DISHES

GREEN CHILI CHICKEN STACKED ENCHILADAS

~

SERVES **6** • SLOW COOKER TIME **5** TO **6** HOURS

The first time I went to Santa Fe, I fell in love with green chiles. Every cook in New Mexico has his or her own version of green chile sauce, and it's served at every meal—with eggs, burritos, roasted chicken, and in enchiladas, as in this recipe. The layers stack up pretty high in the slow cooker, but don't worry; the ingredients will cook down and meld into one cheesy, melt-in-your-mouth dish.

1 TABLESPOON OLIVE OIL

1 ONION, DICED

4 CUPS COOKED CHICKEN, SHREDDED

1 TEASPOON GROUND CUMIN

1 TEASPOON CHILI POWDER

2 (15-OUNCE) CANS GREEN ENCHILADA SAUCE

9–10 TORTILLAS

3 CUPS GRATED CHEDDAR CHEESE

DICED TOMATOES, CHOPPED CILANTRO, AND SOUR CREAM, FOR SERVING

In a medium skillet, heat the olive oil over medium-high. Add the onion and cook, stirring occasionally, until tender and caramelized, about 10 minutes.

In a large bowl, toss the chicken with the cumin and chili powder.

In a slow cooker, pour in about ¼ can of enchilada sauce, spreading evenly across the bottom. Place a tortilla in the slow cooker on top of the sauce. Pour a bit of the sauce on top. Sprinkle on some of the chicken mixture, then some caramelized onions, followed by some cheese. Top with another tortilla. Repeat this process, gently pressing down the layers to compress them and help them stay together (don't worry, the layers will shrink down as they cook). Top the final tortilla with any remaining enchilada sauce and cheddar.

Cover and cook on low for 5 to 6 hours, until the cheese has melted and the enchilada is warmed through. Serve with diced tomatoes, chopped cilantro, and sour cream.

MAIN DISHES

WHITE BEAN AND CORN CHICKEN CHILI

~

SERVE **8** • SLOW COOKER TIME **4 HOURS**

For something a little lighter, this chicken chili fills the bill. It makes a nice change of pace on game night when you still want something hearty, but not too heavy. Mash half the beans before cooking (alternatively, you can purée them in a blender or food processor if you want smoother results) to thicken up the chili and give it more body.

2 (15-OUNCE) CANS GREAT NORTHERN BEANS OR OTHER WHITE BEANS, RINSED AND DRAINED, DIVIDED

2 POUNDS BONELESS, SKINLESS CHICKEN THIGHS, CUBED

1 (10-OUNCE) BAG FROZEN CORN

1 YELLOW ONION, DICED

2 (4-OUNCE) CANS GREEN CHILES, CHOPPED

1 (14-OUNCE) CAN DICED TOMATOES, DRAINED

3 CUPS CHICKEN BROTH

1 TEASPOON GARLIC POWDER

1 TEASPOON CHILI POWDER

1 TEASPOON GROUND CUMIN

1 TEASPOON SALT

CHOPPED CILANTRO, FOR GARNISH (OPTIONAL)

Place half the beans in the slow cooker and gently smash them using a wooden spoon or a potato masher. Add the remaining beans, chicken, corn, onion, green chiles, and diced tomatoes and stir together to combine. Stir in the broth, garlic powder, chili powder, cumin, and salt.

Cover and cook on high for 4 hours, or until the chicken is cooked through. Taste for seasoning and top with chopped cilantro before serving, if desired.

ROSEMARY WHITE BEAN STEW

SERVES **6** TO **8** • SLOW COOKER **8** TO **9** HOURS

I love vegetables—the more, the better—and this stew certainly satisfies all my cravings. The protein-rich beans ensure this stew is filling, and lots of leafy greens (you'll stir them in at the end to retain their texture and color) make it wholesome as well.

1 POUND DRIED WHITE BEANS, SORTED AND RINSED

1 LARGE CARROT, PEELED AND DICED

2 CELERY STALKS, DICED

1 ONION, DICED

3 GARLIC CLOVES, MINCED

1 BAY LEAF

2 TEASPOONS DRIED ROSEMARY

1 (28-OUNCE) CAN DICED TOMATOES

4 CUPS VEGETABLE BROTH

2 TEASPOONS SALT

½ TEASPOON FRESHLY GROUND BLACK PEPPER

5 CUPS ROUGHLY CHOPPED SWISS CHARD, SPINACH, OR KALE LEAVES (TOUGH STEMS DISCARDED)

1 TABLESPOON RED WINE VINEGAR

In a slow cooker, add the beans, carrot, celery, onion, garlic, bay leaf, rosemary, tomatoes and their juices, vegetable broth, salt, and pepper.

Cover and cook on low for 8 to 9 hours, or until the beans are tender. Stir in the chopped greens and let them wilt. Stir in the red wine vinegar and taste for seasoning.

CREAMY MACARONI AND CHEESE

~

SERVES **6** • SLOW COOKER TIME **3 HOURS**

Macaroni and cheese is difficult to make in a slow cooker; it's hard to get that creamy texture that's essential to a good mac and cheese. I know, because I've failed many times. The secret? A can of condensed cheddar cheese soup. The stabilizers that are added to the soup help maintain that all-important creaminess in the slow cooker. I like to garnish with scallions for a bit of extra freshness and color.

1 (10.75-OUNCE) CAN CONDENSED CHEDDAR CHEESE SOUP

2 CUPS WHOLE MILK

2 (12-OUNCE) CANS EVAPORATED MILK

2 TABLESPOONS UNSALTED BUTTER, MELTED

2 TEASPOONS WORCESTERSHIRE SAUCE

1 TEASPOON MUSTARD POWDER

1 TEASPOON SALT

½ TEASPOON FRESHLY GROUND BLACK PEPPER

2 CUPS SHREDDED SHARP CHEDDAR CHEESE

1 CUP SHREDDED MONTEREY JACK CHEESE

2 GARLIC CLOVES, MINCED

1 POUND MACARONI, SMALL PASTA SHELLS, OR OTHER SHORT PASTA

SLICED SCALLIONS, FOR GARNISH (OPTIONAL)

Spray the inside of a slow cooker with cooking spray.

In a large bowl, whisk together the condensed cheddar cheese soup, whole milk, evaporated milk, melted butter, Worcestershire, mustard powder, salt, and pepper. Stir in the shredded cheddar, shredded Monterey Jack, and garlic. Stir in the macaroni. Pour the pasta mixture into the slow cooker.

Cover and cook on high for 30 minutes. Reduce the heat to low and cook for another 2½ hours. Serve garnished with sliced scallions, if desired.

SWEET POTATO AND BEAN VEGGIE CHILI

SERVES **6** • SLOW COOKER TIME **7 HOURS**

This vegetarian chili is anything but boring, and it's just as hearty as one made with meat—you won't miss the beef at all. It has a slightly sweet flavor profile, which comes naturally from the sweet potatoes. If you want more heat in this chili, leave the seeds in one of the jalapeños—I find this adds a nice balance of spice.

2 SWEET POTATOES, PEELED AND DICED INTO ½-INCH PIECES

1 (15.5-OUNCE) CAN PINTO BEANS, RINSED AND DRAINED

1 (15.5-OUNCE) CAN KIDNEY BEANS, RINSED AND DRAINED

1 ONION, DICED

1 GREEN BELL PEPPER, DICED

2 JALAPEÑOS, SEEDED AND MINCED

6 GARLIC CLOVES, MINCED

1 TABLESPOON CHILI POWDER

1 TABLESPOON GROUND CUMIN

2 TEASPOONS UNSWEETENED COCOA POWDER

1 TEASPOON SALT

½ TEASPOON FRESHLY GROUND BLACK PEPPER

1 (28-OUNCE) CAN DICED TOMATOES

1½ CUPS VEGETABLE BROTH

SLICED RADISHES, SLICED SCALLIONS, AND SOUR CREAM, FOR SERVING

In a slow cooker, stir together the sweet potatoes, pinto and kidney beans, onion, bell pepper, jalapeños, garlic, chili powder, cumin, cocoa powder, salt, and black pepper. Stir in the diced tomatoes with their juices and the vegetable broth.

Cover and cook on low for 7 hours, or until the vegetables are tender. Taste for seasoning and serve with the sliced radishes, scallions, and sour cream.

HOPPIN' JOHN

~

SERVES 6 TO 8 • SLOW COOKER TIME 8 TO 9 HOURS

Hoppin' John is traditionally served in the South on New Year's Day for good luck. This version is vegetarian (if using vegetable broth), but many recipes call for bacon as well (and you can certainly add some cooked bacon at the start of this recipe if you're missing the meat). Serve over white rice to soak up all the luscious juices and have a bottle of hot sauce handy to spice things up.

1 POUND DRIED BLACK-EYED PEAS, SORTED AND RINSED

1 GREEN BELL PEPPER, DICED

1 YELLOW ONION, DICED

2 STALKS CELERY, DICED

3 GARLIC CLOVES, MINCED

5 CUPS VEGETABLE OR CHICKEN BROTH

2 BAY LEAVES

2 TEASPOONS CAJUN SEASONING

½ TEASPOON DRIED THYME

1 TEASPOON CAYENNE PEPPER

½ TEASPOON SALT

¼ TEASPOON FRESHLY GROUND BLACK PEPPER

SLICED SCALLIONS, FOR GARNISH

COOKED WHITE RICE, FOR SERVING

HOT SAUCE, FOR SERVING (OPTIONAL)

In a slow cooker, combine the black-eyed peas, bell pepper, onion, celery, and garlic. Stir in the broth, bay leaves, Cajun seasoning, thyme, cayenne, salt, and black pepper.

Cover and cook on low for 8 to 9 hours, or until the peas are tender. Taste for seasoning. Garnish with scallions and serve over rice, with hot sauce on the side if desired.

JAMBALAYA

∿

SERVES **6** • SLOW COOKER TIME **3 HOURS 15 MINUTES**

Every time I visit New Orleans, I'm in awe of the cuisine. You'll find amazing food there that you can't get anywhere else—po'boys, muffalettas, beignets, crawfish étouffée; the list goes on and on. Jambalaya is another uniquely Louisiana specialty. While the rice is often served separately, in this recipe the rice cooks in the slow cooker with the rest of the ingredients to make it a true one-pot meal. Add the raw shrimp at the very end and cook for about 15 minutes, depending on the size of your shrimp; you don't want to overcook it, as it'll turn mealy and mushy.

1 POUND ANDOUILLE SAUSAGE, SLICED ¼-INCH THICK

1 YELLOW ONION, DICED

1 GREEN BELL PEPPER, DICED

3 CELERY STALKS, DICED

4 GARLIC CLOVES, MINCED

1 (28-OUNCE) CAN DICED TOMATOES

2 CUPS CHICKEN BROTH

2 TEASPOONS DRIED THYME

½ TEASPOON CAYENNE PEPPER

1½ TEASPOONS SALT

¾ TEASPOON FRESHLY GROUND BLACK PEPPER

2 CUPS INSTANT RICE

1½ POUNDS SHRIMP, PEELED AND DEVEINED

¼ CUP CHOPPED PARSLEY, PLUS MORE FOR GARNISH (OPTIONAL)

In a slow cooker, combine the sausage, onion, bell pepper, celery, garlic, tomatoes and their juices, broth, thyme, cayenne, salt, and black pepper. Cover and cook on high for 2 hours, or until the vegetables have softened.

Stir in the instant rice. Cover and cook on high for 1 hour, or until the rice has absorbed much of the liquid and is tender. Stir in the shrimp and chopped parsley. Cover and cook on high for 15 minutes, or until the shrimp has turned pink and is cooked through. Taste for seasoning and serve garnished with more parsley, if desired.

DO-IT-YOURSELF PORK TACOS

~

SERVES **10** TO **12** • SLOW COOKER TIME **8** TO **9 HOURS**

Start with this succulent shredded pork and you can build all kinds of wonderful tacos. I like to set out an assortment of toppings—radishes, avocado, cheese, cilantro, tomatoes, shredded lettuce—and let guests assemble their own. It's more fun for your diners, and less work for you.

1 (16-OUNCE) JAR MILD SALSA

1 TABLESPOON GROUND CUMIN

1 TEASPOON CHILI POWDER

1 TEASPOON ONION POWDER

1 TEASPOON PAPRIKA

1 TEASPOON DRIED OREGANO

3 GARLIC CLOVES, MINCED

1 TABLESPOON SALT

4 POUNDS BONELESS PORK SHOULDER

CORN TORTILLAS, FOR SERVING

YOUR FAVORITE TACO GARNISHES, SUCH AS SLICED RADISHES, SLICED AVOCADO, CRUMBLED COTIJA CHEESE, FRESH CILANTRO SPRIGS, OR LIME WEDGES, FOR SERVING

In a slow cooker, pour the salsa evenly into the bottom.

In a small bowl, combine the cumin, chili powder, onion powder, paprika, oregano, garlic, and salt. Rub the mixture all over the pork.

Place the pork in the slow cooker. Cover and cook on low for 8 to 9 hours, or until the pork is very tender.

Using two forks, shred the pork and mix it back into the sauce. Serve with tortillas and taco garnishes.

MAIN DISHES

CHINESE CHICKEN AND BROCCOLI

~

SERVES **6** • SLOW COOKER TIME **3 HOURS**

I grew up eating Chinese food almost every day, but most Asian recipes involve quick cooking over high heat on the stovetop. It's a fun change of pace to use the "set it and forget it" technique with a Chinese dish. The hoisin and soy sauce combine to create an intense sauce that elevates the humble chicken and broccoli; serve with white rice to sop everything up.

¼ CUP HOISIN SAUCE

¼ CUP SOY SAUCE

¼ CUP RICE WINE VINEGAR

1 TABLESPOON SUGAR

2 GARLIC CLOVES, MINCED

1 TEASPOON CRUSHED RED PEPPER FLAKES

2 POUNDS BONELESS, SKINLESS CHICKEN THIGHS, CUT INTO 1½-INCH PIECES

2 TABLESPOONS CORNSTARCH

2 HEADS BROCCOLI, CUT INTO BITE-SIZE FLORETS

COOKED RICE, FOR SERVING

In a slow cooker, whisk together the hoisin, soy sauce, vinegar, sugar, garlic, red pepper flakes, and ¼ cup water. Add the chicken and toss to coat with the sauce. Cover and cook on low for 2 hours.

In a small bowl, whisk together the cornstarch with 2 tablespoons water.

When the chicken has cooked for 2 hours, stir the cornstarch mixture into the slow cooker to thicken the sauce. Add the broccoli florets and toss gently to coat. Cover and cook on high for 1 hour, or until the broccoli is tender. Serve over rice.

MAIN DISHES

93

SOUTHERN PULLED PORK
SANDWICHES

～

SERVES **10** TO **12** • SLOW COOKER TIME **8** TO **9** HOURS

I like to use soft, squishy potato rolls for these sandwiches—the better to sop up the sweet, tangy sauce. The fall-apart pork, sauce, and bread are delicious enough on their own, but I love the briny bite of dill pickles, plus a generous dash of hot sauce. So good!

½ CUP KETCHUP

⅓ CUP CIDER VINEGAR

¼ CUP BROWN SUGAR

¼ CUP TOMATO PASTE

2 TABLESPOONS
WORCESTERSHIRE SAUCE

2 TABLESPOONS PREPARED
MUSTARD

1 YELLOW ONION, DICED

1½ TEASPOONS SALT

1 TEASPOON FRESHLY
GROUND BLACK PEPPER

4 POUNDS BONELESS PORK
SHOULDER

POTATO ROLLS OR
HAMBURGER BUNS, SPLIT,
FOR SERVING

SLICED DILL PICKLES AND
HOT SAUCE, FOR SERVING
(OPTIONAL)

In a slow cooker, stir together the ketchup, vinegar, brown sugar, tomato paste, Worcestershire, mustard, onion, salt, and pepper. Add the pork and turn to coat thoroughly with the sauce.

Cover and cook on low for 8 to 9 hours, or until the pork is very tender.

Using two forks, shred the pork, mixing the meat into the sauce. Taste for seasoning. Let stand uncovered for about 20 minutes.

To assemble a sandwich, pile some of the pulled pork on a potato roll bottom; add pickles and a drizzle of hot sauce, if desired. Close with the potato roll top.

MAIN DISHES

95

PESTO STUFFED SHELLS

~

SERVES **6 TO 8** • SLOW COOKER TIME **3 HOURS**

A warm bowl of cheesy, saucy pasta is great for the soul; it's a worthy meal for any type of celebration. For these shells, you'll add a summery touch by filling them with fresh pesto. Using store-bought pesto is fine (you can find it in the refrigerated section), or make your own—it only takes a couple minutes in the food processor.

1 (12-OUNCE) PACKAGE JUMBO PASTA SHELLS

2 CUPS RICOTTA

1 CUP FRESH PESTO

2 CUPS SHREDDED MOZZARELLA CHEESE

3 LARGE EGGS

2 (24-OUNCE) JARS MARINARA SAUCE

CHOPPED BASIL, FOR GARNISH (OPTIONAL)

In a large pot of boiling salted water, cook the shells according to the instructions on the box until barely al dente. Drain and set aside.

In a large bowl, mix the ricotta, pesto, mozzarella, and eggs.

Pour ½ jar of marinara sauce into the bottom of a slow cooker, spreading evenly.

Take a pasta shell and stuff the inside with about 1 heaping tablespoon of ricotta mixture. Place the stuffed shell in the slow cooker. Repeat with the remaining shells and ricotta mixture.

Pour 1 jar of marinara sauce over the stuffed shells. Cover and cook on high for 3 hours. Pour the remaining ½ jar of sauce into the slow cooker and allow to heat through. Garnish with chopped basil if desired.

SPINACH LASAGNA ROLLUPS

~

SERVES **6** • SLOW COOKER TIME **3 HOURS**

Change up your typical pasta casserole with these fun vegetarian lasagna rollups—they're like individually portioned mini lasagnas. The pasta tends to soak up a lot of the liquid while it cooks, so you'll want to reserve about a half jar of marinara sauce to add at the end for a properly saucy dish.

1 POUND LASAGNA NOODLES (NOT NO-BOIL)

1 (16-OUNCE) CONTAINER RICOTTA

2 CUPS SHREDDED MOZZARELLA

½ CUP GRATED PARMESAN

1 TABLESPOON ITALIAN SEASONING

2 LARGE EGGS

1 (10-OUNCE) PACKAGE FROZEN CHOPPED SPINACH, THAWED AND EXCESS WATER SQUEEZED OUT

2 (24-OUNCE) JARS MARINARA SAUCE, DIVIDED

In a large pot of boiling salted water, cook the lasagna noodles according to the instructions on the box until barely al dente. Drain and set aside.

Meanwhile, in a large bowl, mix the ricotta, mozzarella, Parmesan, Italian seasoning, and eggs. Stir in the spinach.

Pour ½ jar of marinara sauce into the bottom of a slow cooker, spreading evenly.

Cut each lasagna noodle in half crosswise. Spread about 1 heaping tablespoon ricotta mixture across one noodle half. Roll up the noodle and place it in the slow cooker, seam-side down. Continue with the remaining noodles and ricotta mixture.

Pour 1 jar of marinara sauce over the top of the rollups. Cover and cook on high for 3 hours. Pour the remaining ½ jar of sauce into the slow cooker and allow to heat through before serving.

SPANISH RICE WITH HAM AND OLIVES

~

SERVES **6** • SLOW COOKER TIME **3 HOURS**

One-pot rice dishes are a busy cook's best friend. The instant rice cooks directly in the slow cooker, so there's no need to prepare a separate portion. Rice is my comfort food—a big bowl mixed with meat and veggies never fails to make me happy. The combination of ham, olives, and paprika adds a Spanish twist.

1   YELLOW ONION, DICED

1   GREEN BELL PEPPER, DICED

3   GARLIC CLOVES, MINCED

1   CUP CHOPPED COOKED HAM

1   CUP SLICED GREEN PIMENTO-STUFFED OLIVES

2   TEASPOONS PAPRIKA

½   TEASPOON SALT

1   (14.5-OUNCE) CAN DICED TOMATOES

2   CUPS CHICKEN BROTH OR VEGETABLE BROTH

2   CUPS INSTANT WHITE RICE

¼   CUP CHOPPED PARSLEY, PLUS MORE FOR GARNISH (OPTIONAL)

In a slow cooker, combine the onion, bell pepper, garlic, ham, olives, paprika, salt, diced tomatoes and their juices, and broth. Cover and cook on high for 2 hours, or until the vegetables have softened.

Stir in the instant rice. Cover and cook on high for 1 hour, or until the rice has absorbed much of the liquid and is tender. Stir in the chopped parsley; allow to warm through. Taste for seasoning and serve garnished with more parsley, if desired.

SAUSAGE AND CHEESE BREAKFAST CASSEROLE

~

SERVES **6** TO **8** • SLOW COOKER TIME **4 HOURS**

When I'm hosting a group brunch, I nearly always serve a breakfast casserole with eggs, bread, cheese, and a variety of meats or vegetables. It's filling, foolproof, and always a crowd-pleaser. You can customize the ingredients any way you like—experiment with different sausages, change up the veggies, whatever tickles your fancy. Your guests will be clamoring for the recipe.

1 TABLESPOON VEGETABLE OIL

1 POUND SWEET OR HOT ITALIAN SAUSAGE, CASINGS REMOVED

12 LARGE EGGS

2½ CUPS WHOLE MILK

2 TEASPOONS DIJON MUSTARD

1 TEASPOON SALT

½ TEASPOON FRESHLY GROUND BLACK PEPPER

6 CUPS CUBED BAGUETTE (1-INCH CUBES)

1 CUP SHREDDED CHEDDAR CHEESE

1 CUP SHREDDED MONTEREY JACK CHEESE

1 RED BELL PEPPER, DICED

4 SCALLIONS, SLICED

Spray the inside of a slow cooker with cooking spray.

In a large skillet, heat the vegetable oil over medium-high heat. Add the sausage and cook, breaking it up with a spatula, until browned, about 10 minutes. Set aside.

In a very large bowl, whisk together the eggs, milk, mustard, salt, and black pepper. Stir in the bread, allowing it to soak up the liquid. Stir in the cheddar, Monterey Jack, bell pepper, scallions, and sausage. Pour the mixture into the slow cooker.

Cover and cook for 4 hours on high. Remove the lid and let stand about 20 minutes before serving.

CHAPTER 5

DESSERTS
&
SWEETS

CORNMEAL PEACH COBBLER

~

SERVES **8** TO **10** • SLOW COOKER TIME **4 HOURS**

The unusual cornmeal topping gives this summery favorite a Southern twist. Fresh peaches are best, but if they're not in season, frozen sliced peaches make a fine substitute.

3 POUNDS PEACHES, FRESH OR FROZEN AND THAWED, SLICED ¼-INCH THICK

1 CUP SUGAR, DIVIDED

1½ TEASPOONS SALT, DIVIDED

1½ CUPS ALL-PURPOSE FLOUR

¾ CUP CORNMEAL

1 TABLESPOON BAKING POWDER

1¼ CUPS WHOLE MILK

½ CUP UNSALTED BUTTER, MELTED

VANILLA ICE CREAM OR WHIPPED CREAM, FOR SERVING (OPTIONAL)

In a slow cooker, toss the peaches with ¼ cup sugar and ½ teaspoon salt.

In a large bowl, whisk together the flour, cornmeal, baking powder, remaining ¾ cup sugar, and remaining teaspoon salt. Whisk in the milk, then the butter. Pour the batter over the peaches.

Cover and cook on high for 4 hours, or until the cobbler top has puffed up and turned golden at the edges. Serve with ice cream or whipped cream if desired.

APPLE CRISP

~

SERVES 8 • SLOW COOKER TIME 2 HOURS

Every year when fall hits, I make sure to head out to an orchard and spend a day picking apples (and eating cider donuts and drinking fresh-pressed cider). I tend to go a little overboard when it comes to picking fruit; I have so much fun that I always wind up with several pounds of apples. This crisp is the perfect way to put some of them to good use. It comes together wonderfully in a slow cooker; the apples break down gradually and release their sweet juices, while the buttery oats bake up into a deliciously spiced topping. I like to use firm Granny Smith apples, which will hold their shape and add some tartness, but other baking varieties will work just as well.

2 POUNDS GRANNY SMITH OR OTHER BAKING APPLES, PEELED, CORED, AND SLICED ½-INCH THICK	In a slow cooker, arrange the apples in an even layer.
⅔ CUP OLD-FASHIONED OATS	In a medium bowl, combine the oats, flour, brown sugar, cinnamon, and nutmeg. Cut in the butter using two knives or a pastry cutter until the mixture is crumbly. Sprinkle over the apples.
⅔ CUP ALL-PURPOSE FLOUR	
⅔ CUP BROWN SUGAR	Cover and cook on high for 2 hours, or until the apples are tender. Serve with vanilla ice cream or whipped cream if desired.
2 TEASPOONS GROUND CINNAMON	
1 TEASPOON GROUND NUTMEG	
½ CUP UNSALTED BUTTER, CUT INTO PIECES	
VANILLA ICE CREAM OR WHIPPED CREAM, FOR SERVING (OPTIONAL)	

STUFFED SPICED APPLES

~

SERVES **6** • SLOW COOKER TIME **3 HOURS**

Stuffed with a combination of chopped pecans, raisins, brown sugar, and cinnamon, apples transform into an elegant dessert that tastes just like fall. Granny Smith apples are nice and firm, so they'll hold their shape well as they cook.

½ CUP COARSELY CHOPPED PECANS

½ CUP RAISINS

5 TABLESPOONS PLUS 1 CUP BROWN SUGAR, DIVIDED

1 TEASPOON GROUND CINNAMON, DIVIDED

6 MEDIUM GRANNY SMITH APPLES, CORED

¾ CUP APPLE CIDER OR JUICE

In a small bowl, combine the pecans, raisins, 5 tablespoons brown sugar, and ½ teaspoon cinnamon.

Using a peeler or paring knife, peel the skin off the top third of each apple. Place the apples in a single layer in a slow cooker. Spoon the pecan-raisin mixture into the cavity of each apple.

In a small bowl, mix the remaining ½ teaspoon cinnamon, 1 cup brown sugar, and apple cider or juice. Pour the mixture over the apples.

Cover and cook on low for 3 hours, or until the apples are tender. Serve each apple drizzled with the cooking liquid.

STRAWBERRY SHORTCAKE

~

SERVES **8** • SLOW COOKER TIME **2 HOURS 30 MINUTES**

Many people only use their slow cookers during fall and winter, but it's a great year-round appliance. This recipe is a perfect example. You might think it's strange to use a slow cooker for a summer dessert like strawberry shortcake, but it actually makes a lot of sense. The "shortcake" bakes up in the slow cooker right on top of the strawberries, so there's no need to turn on your oven on a hot summer day.

FOR THE STRAWBERRIES:

2 POUNDS STRAWBERRIES, HULLED AND SLICED ¼ INCH THICK

¾ CUP SUGAR

FOR THE SHORTCAKE:

¾ CUP ALL-PURPOSE FLOUR

2½ TEASPOONS BAKING POWDER

½ TEASPOON SALT

1 TEASPOON GROUND CINNAMON

2 TABLESPOONS SUGAR

⅓ CUP WHOLE MILK

2 TABLESPOONS UNSALTED BUTTER, MELTED

WHIPPED CREAM, FOR SERVING

In a slow cooker, gently toss the strawberries with ¾ cup sugar.

In a large bowl, whisk together the flour, baking powder, salt, cinnamon, and 2 tablespoons sugar. Whisk in the milk, then the butter. Drop tablespoons of dough on top of the strawberries, spacing them out evenly.

Cover and cook on high for 2½ hours, or until the shortcake mixture has puffed up. Serve each shortcake with a portion of strawberries and a dollop of whipped cream.

WINE-POACHED PEARS

⁓

SERVES **10** • SLOW COOKER TIME **2 HOURS 30 MINUTES**

This incredibly simple yet sophisticated dessert is a natural for the slow cooker. There's plenty of cooking liquid left over, which I like to drink on its own. It's essentially pear-infused mulled wine—a delicious bonus! If you want a thicker sauce for the pears, you can also transfer some of the cooking liquid to a saucepan on the stove and boil until it reduces and thickens to your liking. Drizzle the syrup over the pears before serving.

1 BOTTLE FRUITY RED WINE (I LIKE TO USE SHIRAZ OR MALBEC)

1 CUP SUGAR

1 TEASPOON WHOLE CLOVES

1 CINNAMON STICK

5 FIRM BUT RIPE PEARS, PEELED, HALVED, AND CORED, STEMS LEFT INTACT

VANILLA ICE CREAM OR WHIPPED CREAM, FOR SERVING

In a slow cooker, stir together the wine, sugar, cloves, and cinnamon. Add the pear halves, submerging them flat-side down in the wine. If necessary, add water to ensure the pears are just covered with liquid.

Cover and cook on high for 2½ hours, or until the pears are tender enough to be pierced with a fork. Serve each pear half with vanilla ice cream or whipped cream drizzled with some of the cooking liquid.

BANANAS FOSTER

∼

SERVES **12** • SLOW COOKER TIME **1 HOUR**

Created at the legendary Brennan's in New Orleans, this classic dessert takes almost no effort to make in a slow cooker. The buttery rum-spiked sauce is intensely delectable, especially when drizzled over that all-important scoop of vanilla ice cream.

6 MEDIUM, FIRM BANANAS, PEELED

¾ CUP BROWN SUGAR

¼ CUP UNSALTED BUTTER, MELTED

¼ CUP DARK RUM

2 TEASPOONS VANILLA EXTRACT

1 TEASPOON GROUND CINNAMON

VANILLA ICE CREAM, FOR SERVING

Cut the bananas in half lengthwise, then widthwise. Layer them in the bottom of a slow cooker.

In a small bowl, whisk together the brown sugar, butter, rum, vanilla, and cinnamon. Pour over the bananas.

Cover and cook on low for 1 hour. Serve the bananas with vanilla ice cream drizzled with the rum sauce.

DESSERTS & SWEETS

STEWED FRUIT COMPOTE

~

SERVES **6** TO **8** • SLOW COOKER TIME **2** TO **3** HOURS

This lovely dish makes a wonderfully different dessert. The dried fruit plumps up and softens in the slow cooker, creating a luscious, cinnamon-infused sauce. There's no need to add extra sugar—the fruit is sweet enough on its own. Have leftover compote? Serve it for breakfast the next morning with some Greek yogurt and granola for a decadent start to the day.

¾ POUND PRUNES

¾ POUND DRIED APRICOTS

½ CUP GOLDEN RAISINS

2 APPLES, PEELED, CORED, AND SLICED ¼-INCH THICK

2 TEASPOONS GROUND CINNAMON

¼ CUP FRESH ORANGE JUICE

2 TABLESPOONS FRESH LEMON JUICE

MASCARPONE OR PLAIN GREEK YOGURT, FOR SERVING

In a slow cooker, combine the prunes, apricots, raisins, apples, cinnamon, and orange juice with 2 cups of water; stir well.

Cover and cook on low for 2 to 3 hours, or until the fruit is tender. Stir in the fresh lemon juice. Serve topped with a dollop of mascarpone or Greek yogurt.

BANANA CARAMEL CAKE

~

SERVES **8 TO 10** • SLOW COOKER TIME **1 HOUR 30 MINUTES**

When I first visited Argentina, I became obsessed with dulce de leche, a caramel sauce typically made from milk and sugar that you'll find in a lot of desserts and sweets there. I decided to incorporate it into this tempting banana cake, enriched with molasses and swirled with caramel. If you can find dulce de leche in your supermarket or specialty food store, it's worth the splurge. Avoid "caramel-flavored" sauces, which are full of artificial flavors and colors.

6 TABLESPOONS UNSALTED BUTTER, SOFTENED

⅔ CUP SUGAR

2 LARGE EGGS

2 TABLESPOONS MOLASSES

1¾ CUPS ALL-PURPOSE FLOUR

2 TEASPOONS BAKING POWDER

¼ TEASPOON BAKING SODA

½ TEASPOON SALT

3 RIPE BANANAS, MASHED

1 CUP DULCE DE LECHE OR CARAMEL SAUCE

Spray the inside of a slow cooker with cooking spray.

In a medium bowl, cream together the butter and sugar using a handheld mixer or standing mixer. Beat in the eggs and molasses.

In a large bowl, whisk together the flour, baking powder, baking soda, and salt. Add the flour mixture to the butter mixture in batches, beating in between each addition. Stir in the bananas.

Pour the batter into the slow cooker, spreading evenly. Drizzle the dulce de leche on top and swirl into the batter with a knife. Cover and cook on high for 1½ hours, or until the cake is set. Let cool for about 20 minutes uncovered before serving.

WARM TIRAMISU

~

SERVES 8 • SLOW COOKER TIME 3 TO 4 HOURS

Serving tiramisu for dessert is always a win; I haven't met anyone who doesn't love it. Making it in the slow cooker adds an extra "wow" factor for friends and family. For the optimal tiramisu experience, be generous with the whipped mascarpone topping and the cocoa powder before serving.

FOR THE TIRAMISU:

1 CUP SUGAR

2 TABLESPOONS INSTANT ESPRESSO POWDER

5 TABLESPOONS KAHLÚA

3 CUPS WHOLE MILK

1 CUP HEAVY CREAM

9 LARGE EGGS

2 (7-OUNCE) PACKAGES LADYFINGERS OR 8 CUPS CUBED BREAD

FOR THE TOPPING:

1 CUP HEAVY CREAM

½ CUP MASCARPONE

2 TABLESPOONS SUGAR

2 TEASPOONS VANILLA EXTRACT

UNSWEETENED COCOA POWDER, FOR GARNISH

Spray the inside of a slow cooker with cooking spray.

Make the tiramisu: In a small saucepan, combine the sugar and espresso powder with 1 cup water. Cook over medium heat, stirring, until the sugar and espresso powder have dissolved. Remove from the heat, stir in the Kahlúa, and let cool for 15 minutes.

In a very large bowl, whisk together the milk, cream, and eggs. Whisk in the cooled espresso mixture. Working in batches, add the ladyfingers to the mixture and let them soak up the liquid. Once the ladyfingers are soaked, use a slotted spoon to transfer them to the slow cooker, spreading evenly. Pour any remaining liquid over the top of the ladyfingers. Cover and cook on low 3 to 4 hours, or until the tiramisu is set. Let sit, uncovered, for 20 minutes.

Make the topping: In a large bowl, whip the cream, mascarpone, sugar, and vanilla using a stand mixer or handheld mixer until soft peaks form.

Serve the tiramisu with a large dollop of the mascarpone whipped cream, dusted with unsweetened cocoa powder.

CHOCOLATE PEANUT BUTTER CAKE

SERVES **8** • SLOW COOKER TIME **4 HOURS**

I never had an Easy-Bake oven as a kid, which I think is why I'm so smitten with baking in a slow cooker. This one-bowl cake is super easy; just mix all the ingredients together, then let it cook on low for a few hours. If you want an extra chocolaty cake, stir in some chocolate chips along with the peanut butter chips before baking.

2 CUPS ALL-PURPOSE FLOUR

1 TEASPOON BAKING SODA

1 TEASPOON BAKING POWDER

1¼ CUPS SUGAR

6 TABLESPOONS UNSWEETENED DUTCH PROCESS COCOA POWDER

1 TEASPOON SALT

2 LARGE EGGS, BEATEN

1 CUP WHOLE MILK

⅓ CUP CANOLA OIL

1 TEASPOON VANILLA EXTRACT

1½ CUPS PEANUT BUTTER CHIPS

½ CUP CHOCOLATE CHIPS, OPTIONAL

Spray a slow cooker with cooking spray.

In a large bowl, whisk together the flour, baking soda, baking powder, sugar, cocoa powder, and salt. Stir in the eggs, milk, oil, and vanilla, mixing until well-combined. Stir in the peanut butter chips and chocolate chips, if using.

Pour the batter into the slow cooker, spreading evenly. Cover and cook on low for 4 hours, until the top is set. The cake will still look a little undercooked. Turn off the heat and let the cake cool, uncovered, for 20 minutes before serving. The cake will firm up as it cools but should still be moist inside.

S'MORES CASSEROLE

~

SERVES 10 • **SLOW COOKER TIME 2 HOURS**

If there's a fire in the vicinity—be it a wood-burning fireplace, bonfire, or fire pit—you can bet I'm going to rustle up some roasting sticks and make s'mores. I can't get enough of the combination of toasted, gooey marshmallow, melty chocolate, and crunchy graham crackers. Though I'm usually not a fan of using boxed cake mix, I think that cooking s'mores in a slow cooker should be nearly as easy as making the real deal. This cake version of the campfire classic is incredibly decadent and oh-so-good.

3 CUPS GRAHAM CRACKER CRUMBS (ABOUT 24 GRAHAM CRACKERS)

10 TABLESPOONS UNSALTED BUTTER, MELTED

1 (15.25-OUNCE) BOX CHOCOLATE CAKE MIX

EGG AND OIL, AS CALLED FOR ON THE CAKE MIX BOX

1 (12-OUNCE) BAG CHOCOLATE CHIPS

4 CUPS MINI MARSHMALLOWS

Spray the inside of a slow cooker with cooking spray.

In a medium bowl, combine the graham cracker crumbs and butter. Mix well. Press the graham cracker mixture evenly into the bottom of the slow cooker.

Prepare the cake mix according to the instructions on the box. Stir in 1 cup of the chocolate chips. Pour the cake mixture into the slow cooker.

Cover and cook on high for 2 hours, or until the cake is set. Scatter the marshmallows and the remaining chocolate chips over the cake and let melt before serving.

CHOCOLATE CHIP CHEESECAKE

~

SERVES **6** • SLOW COOKER TIME **2 HOURS**

Yes, you can make a fantastic cheesecake in your slow cooker. The dessert doesn't cook directly in the insert; you'll need a 6-inch springform pan (make sure it fits!) to hold your batter. The cake steams in the pan, resulting in a silky-smooth texture.

¾ CUP GRAHAM CRACKER CRUMBS (ABOUT 6–7 GRAHAM CRACKERS)

1 TEASPOON UNSWEETENED COCOA POWDER

½ TEASPOON SALT, DIVIDED

3 TABLESPOONS UNSALTED BUTTER, MELTED

12 OUNCES CREAM CHEESE, SOFTENED

½ CUP SUGAR

1 TABLESPOON ALL-PURPOSE FLOUR

2 LARGE EGGS

1 TEASPOON VANILLA EXTRACT

1 CUP SOUR CREAM

1 CUP SEMISWEET CHOCOLATE CHIPS

In a medium bowl, whisk together the graham cracker crumbs, cocoa powder, and ¼ teaspoon salt. Stir in the butter. Press the crumbs over the bottom and slightly up the sides of a 6-inch springform pan.

In a large bowl, combine the cream cheese, sugar, flour, and ¼ teaspoon salt. Using a standing or handheld mixer, beat the cream cheese mixture at medium-high until smooth, about 2 minutes. Add the eggs one at a time, then the vanilla, then the sour cream, beating at medium speed between each addition until well-blended. Stir in the chocolate chips. Pour the batter into the springform pan.

Fill the slow cooker with about ½ inch of water and place a rack (or an inverted heatproof bowl) in the bottom. Place the pan on the rack. Cover and cook on high for 2 hours. Turn off the heat and let stand, covered, for 1 hour. Remove the cheesecake to a rack and let cool completely. Cover with plastic wrap and refrigerate until chilled, at least 4 hours.

CINNAMON MONKEY BREAD

~

SERVES 8 TO 10 • SLOW COOKER TIME 2 TO 3 HOURS

This pull-apart dessert is as fun to make as it is to eat. It's a great project for kids, too; they can help shake up the sugar and coat the biscuit pieces. Once cooked, the bottom of the monkey bread should be sticky and caramelized, thanks to the leftover melted butter that's poured into the bottom of the slow cooker. Invert the monkey bread onto a platter before serving to reveal the delicious caramel topping.

1 TEASPOON GROUND CINNAMON

½ CUP WHITE SUGAR

½ CUP BROWN SUGAR

1 (16.3-OUNCE) TUBE BISCUIT DOUGH

½ CUP UNSALTED BUTTER, MELTED

Spray the inside of a slow cooker with cooking spray.

In a gallon-size resealable plastic bag, combine the cinnamon, white sugar, and brown sugar; seal the bag and shake thoroughly to mix the ingredients.

Open the biscuit tube and separate the biscuits. Cut each biscuit into 6 equal-size pieces. Place the melted butter in a shallow bowl.

Take a biscuit piece and dip it into the melted butter, then place it into the cinnamon sugar mixture in the resealable plastic bag. Repeat with the remaining biscuit pieces, until all the pieces are in the bag. Seal the bag and shake gently until all the pieces are coated with cinnamon sugar.

Pour any leftover butter into the bottom of the slow cooker. Add the cinnamon sugar-coated biscuit pieces in an even layer on the bottom.

Cover and cook on low for 2 to 3 hours, or until the biscuits have puffed up and cooked through.

LEMON CHEESECAKE

~

SERVES **6** • SLOW COOKER TIME **2 HOURS**

My whole family is crazy for cheesecake; the more flavors and varieties, the better. For something a little lighter, this lemon cheesecake is a nice alternative to the Chocolate Chip Cheesecake (page 122). You'll use the same springform pan and cooking technique for both; it just depends on whether you're in the mood for citrus or chocolate.

¾ CUP GRAHAM CRACKER CRUMBS (ABOUT 6–7 GRAHAM CRACKERS)

3 TABLESPOONS UNSALTED BUTTER, MELTED

½ TEASPOON SALT, DIVIDED

12 OUNCES CREAM CHEESE, SOFTENED

½ CUP SUGAR

1 TABLESPOON ALL-PURPOSE FLOUR

2 LARGE EGGS

JUICE AND ZEST OF 1 LEMON

In a medium bowl, mix the graham cracker crumbs with the melted butter and ¼ teaspoon salt. Press the crumbs over the bottom and slightly up the sides of a 6-inch springform pan.

In a large bowl, add the cream cheese, sugar, flour, and ¼ teaspoon salt. Using a standing or handheld mixer, beat the cream cheese mixture at medium-high until smooth, about 2 minutes. Add the eggs one at a time, then the lemon juice, then the lemon zest, beating at medium speed between each addition until well-blended. Pour the batter into the springform pan.

Fill the slow cooker with about ½ inch of water and place a rack in the bottom (you can also use an inverted heatproof bowl). Place the springform pan on the rack.

Cover and cook on high for 2 hours. Turn off the heat and let stand, covered, for 1 hour. Remove the cheesecake to a rack and let cool completely. Cover with plastic wrap and refrigerate until chilled, at least 4 hours.

MOLTEN CHOCOLATE CAKE

~

SERVES **8** TO **10** • SLOW COOKER TIME **2 HOURS 30 MINUTES**

Making a cake in a slow cooker seems like a magic trick: Put in wet and dry ingredients, cover with a lid, and a few hours later, presto! Out comes a fluffy, moist chocolate cake. This one is special because it creates its own rich, chocolaty sauce as it cooks—no extra effort required.

2 CUPS ALL-PURPOSE FLOUR

2½ CUPS BROWN SUGAR, DIVIDED

6 TABLESPOONS PLUS ½ CUP UNSWEETENED DUTCH PROCESS COCOA POWDER

4 TEASPOONS BAKING POWDER

1 TEASPOON SALT

4 TABLESPOONS UNSALTED BUTTER, MELTED

1 CUP WHOLE MILK

1 TEASPOON VANILLA EXTRACT

1 CUP SEMISWEET CHOCOLATE CHIPS

3 CUPS BOILING WATER

VANILLA ICE CREAM OR WHIPPED CREAM, FOR SERVING

Spray the inside of a slow cooker with cooking spray.

In a large bowl, combine the flour, 1½ cups brown sugar, 6 tablespoons cocoa powder, baking powder, and salt. Stir in the melted butter, milk, and vanilla until thoroughly combined. Stir in the chocolate chips. Pour the batter into the slow cooker, spreading evenly.

In a medium bowl, combine 1 cup brown sugar and ½ cup cocoa powder. Sprinkle the mixture over the cake batter.

Pour the boiling water over the batter. Do not stir into the batter.

Cover and cook on high for 2½ hours. Turn off the heat, remove the lid, and let sit about 20 minutes. Serve with vanilla ice cream or whipped cream.

CHAPTER 6

WARM
DRINKS

MULLED WINE

~

SERVES **8** TO **10** • SLOW COOKER TIME **4 HOURS**

One of my favorite things about the holiday season is the excuse to drink mulled wine—and lots of it. I love how so many cultures have their own tasty version (glögg in Sweden, Glühwein in Austria, vinho quente in Portugal). This version is fortified with brandy and flavored with orange and lemon for a little citrus lift.

1 TEASPOON WHOLE BLACK PEPPERCORNS

6 WHOLE ALLSPICE BERRIES

2 WHOLE STAR ANISE

3 CINNAMON STICKS

3 LARGE STRIPS ORANGE PEEL

3 LARGE STRIPS LEMON PEEL

2 BOTTLES FRUITY RED WINE (I LIKE TO USE SHIRAZ OR MALBEC)

¼ CUP BRANDY

¾ CUP SUGAR

In a double thickness of cheesecloth, place the peppercorns, allspice, star anise, cinnamon sticks, orange peel, and lemon peel. Gather the corners to make a bag and tie securely with kitchen twine.

In a slow cooker, mix the wine, brandy, and sugar. Submerge the spice bag in the liquid.

Cover and cook on high for 4 hours, or until the sugar has dissolved and the spices have infused the liquid. Remove the spice bag and stir before serving.

SPICED APPLE CIDER

~

SERVES **8** • SLOW COOKER TIME **4 HOURS**

Apples and oranges? You don't have to compare them; just combine them in this warm cider simmered with fragrant spices—cinnamon, cloves, and allspice—and slices of orange.

2 CINNAMON STICKS

1 TEASPOON WHOLE CLOVES

1 TEASPOON WHOLE ALLSPICE BERRIES

2 QUARTS APPLE CIDER

¼ CUP BROWN SUGAR

1 ORANGE, SLICED INTO ROUNDS

In a double thickness of cheesecloth, place the cinnamon sticks, cloves, and allspice. Gather the corners to make a bag and tie securely with kitchen twine.

In a slow cooker, mix the apple cider and brown sugar. Submerge the spice bag in the liquid and add the orange slices.

Cover and cook on high for 4 hours, or until the brown sugar has dissolved and the spices have infused the liquid. Remove the spice bag and stir before serving. Serve each drink garnished with an orange slice from the slow cooker.

WINTER SANGRIA

~

SERVES **8** TO **10** • SLOW COOKER TIME **2 HOURS**

Sangria isn't just for summer. This warm winterized version looks beautiful in a glass and is bursting with fruity flavor. I love the cherries in this recipe; they add a sweet-tart juiciness that gives this drink an especially festive touch.

2 BOTTLES FRUITY RED WINE (I LIKE TO USE SHIRAZ OR MALBEC)

1 CUP POMEGRANATE JUICE

½ CUP BRANDY

¼ CUP TRIPLE SEC

¼ CUP SUGAR

1 PEAR, CORED AND THINLY SLICED

1 APPLE, DICED

1 ORANGE, THINLY SLICED

1 BAG FROZEN CHERRIES, THAWED

In a slow cooker, mix all the ingredients. Cover and cook on low for 2 hours, or until the sugar has dissolved and the fruit has softened. Stir and serve each drink garnished with the fruit.

GINGER BOURBON PUNCH

~

SERVES **8 TO 10** • SLOW COOKER TIME **2 HOURS**

Looking for a change from mulled wine and cider? Here's the perfect unexpected (and sophisticated) drink to serve at your next cool-weather cocktail party. There's a nice spicy bite to this warming drink, thanks to the fresh ginger that simmers along with the other ingredients. Fresh lemon juice keeps it bright and cuts down the sweetness.

½   CUP FRESH LEMON JUICE

½   CUP HONEY

1   3-INCH PIECE FRESH
    GINGER, PEELED AND
    THINLY SLICED

3   CUPS FRESH ORANGE
    JUICE

2   CUPS PEAR JUICE

3   CUPS BOURBON

In a slow cooker, mix all the ingredients with 2 cups water. Cover and cook on low for 2 hours, or until the honey has dissolved. Stir before serving.

HONEY BOURBON CIDER

~

SERVES **8 TO 10** • SLOW COOKER TIME **2 HOURS**

This bourbon-spiked cider always earns raves (and recipe requests) when I serve it at parties. Stirring in lemon juice before serving balances out the sweet honey, and the tender apples are delicious eaten on their own, too.

6½ CUPS APPLE CIDER

2½ CUPS BOURBON

3 TABLESPOONS HONEY

½ TEASPOON CINNAMON

1 APPLE, CORED AND THINLY SLICED

1 TABLESPOON FRESH LEMON JUICE

In a slow cooker, mix the cider, bourbon, honey, and cinnamon. Stir in the apple slices.

Cover and cook on low for 2 hours, or until the honey has dissolved and the apples have softened. Stir in the lemon juice and serve.

ORANGE BOURBON PUNCH

~

SERVES **8** • SLOW COOKER TIME **2 HOURS**

Can you tell I love bourbon? It's usually my alcohol of choice when I have a cocktail. This four-ingredient punch couldn't be more effortless; it's a great last-minute drink to throw together for a crowd. It may be simple, but it's quite refreshing and goes down easy.

2 CUPS FRESH ORANGE JUICE

2 CUPS BOURBON

4 CUPS LEMONADE

¼ CUP POMEGRANATE JUICE

In a slow cooker, mix all the ingredients. Cover and cook on low for 2 hours.

CRANBERRY ORANGE PUNCH

~

For a holiday beverage the whole family can enjoy, mix up a batch of this non-alcoholic punch. It's tangy with an undertone of cinnamon that keeps it seasonal. If the grownups decide they need an extra kick, a splash of bourbon or dark rum would be a fantastic addition.

2 QUARTS CRANBERRY JUICE

3 CUPS FRESH ORANGE JUICE

½ CUP BROWN SUGAR

2 TABLESPOONS FRESH LEMON JUICE

2 CINNAMON STICKS

In a slow cooker, mix all the ingredients. Cover and cook on low for 2 hours, or until the sugar has dissolved. Stir before serving.

HOT TODDY

~

SERVES **8** • SLOW COOKER TIME **2 HOURS**

I love a good hot toddy, but ordering one at a bar is often hit or miss—there are so many different ways to make it. Some people make it with tea, some use granulated sugar, and some use Scotch, bourbon, brandy, or another type of alcohol. For me, the ultimate hot toddy must include Irish whiskey, honey, and fresh lemon. I love Jameson, so that's my go-to whiskey for this classic cocktail.

2 CUPS IRISH WHISKEY

½ CUP HONEY

6 CINNAMON STICKS

1 LEMON, THINLY SLICED

In a slow cooker, mix all the ingredients with 5 cups water. Cover and cook on low for 2 hours, or until the honey has dissolved. Stir and serve each drink garnished with a lemon slice from the slow cooker.

RICH HOT CHOCOLATE

~

SERVES 8 • SLOW COOKER TIME 2 TO 3 HOURS

I'm not a big fan of instant hot chocolate mixes, where you simply add hot water and stir. And while I do love a high-quality hot chocolate made with milk and cream, sometimes the ones I've sampled at fancy cafés are so sweet and thick, it's hard to drink more than a few sips. This hot chocolate strikes the perfect balance between the two. There's plenty of richness from all the dairy, but I've added water to thin things out a bit. This drink also has both cocoa powder and chocolate chips, so you're getting a doubly delicious dose of chocolate.

½ CUP UNSWEETENED
COCOA POWDER

6 CUPS WHOLE MILK

1 (14-OUNCE) CAN
SWEETENED CONDENSED
MILK

1 CUP HEAVY CREAM

PINCH OF SALT

1 CUP SEMI-SWEET
CHOCOLATE CHIPS

In a slow cooker, whisk the cocoa, milk, condensed milk, cream, and salt with ⅔ cup water. Stir in the chocolate chips.

Cover and cook on low for 2 to 3 hours, or until the chocolate chips have melted. Whisk thoroughly before serving.

WHITE HOT CHOCOLATE

~

SERVES **8** TO **10** • SLOW COOKER TIME **2** TO **3 HOURS**

I know a lot of "serious" food people look down on white chocolate, but I don't think there's anything wrong with it every so often. For a change of pace from your typical hot chocolate, try this all-white version—it's quite decadent. You can even swap in peppermint oil instead of vanilla extract for a minty holiday twist. Garnish each mug with a candy cane for the full effect.

6 CUPS WHOLE MILK

2 CUPS HEAVY CREAM

1 TEASPOON VANILLA EXTRACT

12 OUNCES WHITE CHOCOLATE, CHOPPED, OR 12 OUNCES WHITE CHOCOLATE CHIPS

In a slow cooker, whisk together the milk, cream, and vanilla. Stir in the white chocolate.

Cover and cook on low for 2 to 3 hours, or until the chocolate has melted. Whisk thoroughly before serving.

SPICY HOT CHOCOLATE

~

This hot chocolate is super delicious and has just the right amount of heat—enough so that you can taste it, but not so much that you need a glass of water afterwards. The cinnamon, nutmeg, and cayenne are really warming; absolutely perfect for a cold winter day.

1½ CUPS HEAVY CREAM

1 (14-OUNCE) CAN SWEETENED CONDENSED MILK

7 CUPS WHOLE MILK

1 TEASPOON VANILLA EXTRACT

1 TEASPOON GROUND CINNAMON

1 TEASPOON GROUND NUTMEG

½ TEASPOON CAYENNE PEPPER

2 CUPS SEMISWEET CHOCOLATE CHIPS

In a slow cooker, whisk together the cream, condensed milk, whole milk, vanilla, cinnamon, nutmeg, and cayenne. Stir in the chocolate chips.

Cover and cook on low for 2 to 3 hours, or until the chocolate has melted. Whisk thoroughly before serving.

CAFÉ AU LAIT

~

SERVES **12** • SLOW COOKER TIME **2 HOURS**

I don't drink coffee every day, but when I do, I usually take it black. When I'm in the mood for a treat, however, I like to indulge in a good café au lait made with lots of creamy, frothy milk. This slow cooker version meant for a crowd makes it easy to serve a special drink at a big brunch or as a post-dinner treat. For those who want a boozy hazelnut kick, add a splash of Frangelico.

5 TABLESPOONS INSTANT COFFEE

8 CUPS WHOLE MILK

In a slow cooker, whisk together the coffee, milk, and 4 cups water. Cover and cook on low for 2 hours.

Use a handheld immersion blender to whip the liquid (be careful, as the liquid is hot) or whisk vigorously by hand until frothy.

SPICED CHAI TEA

~

SERVES **12** • SLOW COOKER TIME **4 HOURS 15 MINUTES**

Tea, not coffee, is my hot drink of choice, so a warm, creamy cup of spiced chai does it for me every time. Store-bought chai lattes are often overly sweet, but the condensed milk in this homemade version adds just the right amount of sweetness. The spices steeping in your slow cooker will make your whole house smell amazing.

2 TEASPOONS WHOLE CLOVES

1 TABLESPOON CARDAMOM PODS, CRUSHED

3 CINNAMON STICKS

6 WHOLE ALLSPICE BERRIES

8 BLACK TEA BAGS

1 (14-OUNCE) CAN SWEETENED CONDENSED MILK

In a double thickness of cheesecloth, place the cloves, cardamom, cinnamon, and allspice. Gather the corners to make a bag and tie securely with kitchen twine.

In a slow cooker, submerge the spice bag in 12 cups water. Cover and cook on high for 4 hours.

Add the tea bags, cover, and continue cooking for another 15 minutes. Remove the tea bags and spice bag. Stir in the condensed milk and allow to heat through before serving.

ACKNOWLEDGMENTS

While I was working on this book, I realized how lucky I am. This cookbook is essentially the culmination of my entire professional career; I went to culinary school and have worked at various companies as a writer, editor, recipe developer, copy editor, and proofreader. Along the way, I've learned how to:

- properly write a recipe
- season my food
- produce a photo shoot
- write compelling recipe headnotes
- style recipes for photos
- proofread cookbooks
- round up props for shoots

. . . and many, many more things. And I used every one of those skills while creating this book.

So first and foremost, I would like to thank everyone I've worked with who has taught me something—from the food stylists I collaborated with on photo shoots to editors who improved my writing to culinary instructors who trained me on how to hold a knife properly. I've learned from each and every one of you.

More specifically: Big thanks to my editor, Ann Treistman, for giving me this opportunity and for being unfailingly supportive, positive, and easy to work with. You and the rest of the amazing team at The Countryman Press made this project as stress-free as producing a cookbook could possibly be.

My photographer, Jonathan Meter, made my food look beautiful, was a blast to work with, and went above and beyond to make sure the results were as gorgeous as possible. You were a true team player and incredibly professional. Thanks also to Jessica Meter for letting us make a mess out of your apartment on numerous occasions.

My family provided invaluable support . . . and didn't give me *too* much grief for working on this book instead of getting a full-time job with benefits. My friends were phenomenal cheerleaders/tasters/eaters of massive quantities of leftovers. Danielle Paige and Vernaliz Co deserve a special shout-out for always encouraging me and pushing me in my creative endeavors. Shirley Fan also provided great advice and guidance. And I couldn't have wrangled all the props for the photos (literally and figuratively) without Jennifer Gillespie's tremendous help.

Most of all, my agent Sharon Bowers deserves a huge thanks for essentially dropping this opportunity in my lap. You walked me through the entire process and gave indispensable advice along the way. This cookbook would not have happened without you.

INDEX

* Italics indicate illustrations